Beyond Stereotypes: American Jews and Sports

The Jewish Role in American Life

An Annual Review of the Casden Institute for the Study of the Jewish Role in American Life

Beyond Stereotypes: American Jews and Sports

The Jewish Role in American Life

An Annual Review of the Casden Institute for the
Study of the Jewish Role in American Life

Volume 12

Bruce Zuckerman, *Editor*
Ari F. Sclar, *Guest Editor*
Lisa Ansell, *Associate Editor*

Published by the Purdue University Press for
the USC Casden Institute for the Study of the
Jewish Role in American Life

© 2014
University of Southern California
Casden Institute for the
Study of the Jewish Role in American Life.
All rights reserved.

First printing in paperback, 2024.

Production Editor, Marilyn Lundberg

Cover photo:
Yochanan Katz.
Courtesy of Larry Palumbo, Coyote Magic Images.

978-1-55753-699-0 (hardcover)
978-1-61249-910-9 (paperback)
978-1-61249-355-8 (epdf)
978-1-61249-356-5 (epub)
ISSN 1934-7529

Published by Purdue University Press
West Lafayette, Indiana
www.thepress.purdue.edu
pupress@purdue.edu

Printed in the United States of America.

For subscription information,
call 1-800-247-6553

Contents

FOREWORD — vii

EDITORIAL INTRODUCTION — ix
Ari F. Sclar, Guest Editor

Joseph Dorinson — 1
A Stack of Jewish Baseball Cards: Some Thoughts on Jews and the Roles They Have Played in the Major Leagues

Rebecca Alpert — 19
Racial Attitudes towards Jews in the "Negro Leagues":
The Case of Effa Manley

Linda J. Borish — 43
American Jewish Women on the Court: Seeking an Identity in Tennis in the Early Decades of the Twentieth Century

Jeffrey S. Gurock — 73
Answering to a Different Authority in Sports: The Trials of Coach Jonathan Halpert and the Limits of Yeshiva University's Athletic Success in Basketball

Ari F. Sclar — 95
"The Disadvantage Far Outweighs the Benefits": How the Rise and Fall of "the Jewish Game" at the 92nd Street YMHA Exemplified Jewish Conceptions of Athleticism

Neil Kramer — 129
From Suburbanites to Sabras and Back: How Jewish Americans Established Lacrosse in Israel

ABOUT THE CONTRIBUTORS — 143

ABOUT THE USC CASDEN INSTITUTE — 147

Foreword

"Wee Willie" Keeler, who played major league baseball a little over a century ago, is now mostly remembered for the sage advice he gave to his fellow batters—"Keep your eye clear, and hit 'em where they ain't" (http://en.wikipedia.org/wiki/Willie_Keeler). I have long thought that such advice not only leads to success in baseball, but also obtains to managing the editing of the Casden *Annual Review*. Counting this edition, I have now guided to publication seven *Annual Reviews*; and, when initially deciding each time what we wanted to do, I have found Wee Willie's advice to come in handy. That is, I have made sure to keep my eyes out for a particularly creative guest editor, around whom a intriguing set of authors and essays might coalesce, and I have also tried to hit on a topic that might at first seem familiar but which we could take another way—like a right-handed batter who slaps a groundball into the unguarded hole between first and second base for a hit.

Thus, when we decided to do Volume 6 on the Holocaust (with guest-editor Zev Garber), we self-consciously went at it from a different slant: the impact of the Holocaust *in America*—an aspect of Holocaust studies that not so many scholars or readers had ever considered. When we examined Jewish cultural history in the United States in Volume 7 (with guest editor Bill Deverell) we did not look east, as is usually done, but rather turned our attention to the southwest where Jews had quite a different experience. When we considered Jews and popular American music in Volume 8 (with guest-editor Josh Kun), we went out of our way to highlight aspects of this topic that had not been much thought about before—as the title of that volume, *The Song Is Not the Same*, indicated. When we looked at the Jewish role in facilitating community diversity in Volume 9 (with guest-editor George Sanchez), we focused on the profiles of southern California figures who were not widely known on the national stage, but who, nonetheless, had made a profound impression on the reshaping of cultural and racial identities and aspirations in the Los Angeles area and beyond. We worked with guest-editor Ruth Weisberg on Volume 10, which considered whether there is (or should be) a modern genre labeled

"Jewish Art." And in Volume 11, guest-editor Dan Schnur brought together a series of demographic studies that gave us a profile of Jewish voters that considered how and why they do not act in a typical fashion—why this voting bloc is different from all other voting blocs.

As the title of this our latest volume emphasizes, our aim continues to be (as it has always been) to get *Beyond Stereotypes*—to get our reading public to look closely at aspects of a seemingly familiar topic, which, when more closely examined, reveals itself to have intriguing aspects that few have previously considered. The Jewish role in sports more than fills the bill. Note, in this respect, the figure on the cover—a lacrosse player with the beard of an observant Jew and an Israeli team-chevron on his uniform. Our aim (of course) in choosing this cover picture is to be intentionally provocative—to induce you to ask, what do Jews have to do with lacrosse or why use an Israeli player as the cover figure, when the Casden Institute is supposed to keep its focus on the Jewish role in *American* life? To find out, you'll just have to read more.

Our guest editor this time around, Ari Sclar, has long been known as the historian who has led the way in considering the study of sports in America, on and off the field, from a distinctly Jewish perspective. I want to take this occasion to thank Prof. Sclar for being such a fine collaborator and for putting together such a fine collection of essays written by such an excellent group of specialists in this less well-considered area of study.

I hope that Alan Casden, an avid sports fan and collector of sports memorabilia, without whose support the Casden Institute would not exist, will find this volume particularly enjoyable. My appreciations also go out to other stalwart supporters of the Casden Institute, year in and year out: Ruth Ziegler, Sam and Mark Tarica, Dean of Dornsife College Steve Kay, Provost Elizabeth Garrett and (batting clean-up) C. L. Max Nikias, President of the University of Southern California.

* * * *

This will be my last at-bat as managing editor of the Casden *Annual Review*. I will be stepping down as Myron and Marion Director of the Casden Institute for the Study of the Jewish Role in American Life as of the start of the next academic year. Next time around my successor as Director, USC Professor of History Steven J. Ross will be guiding the *Annual Review*, and I have no doubt that he will do a superb job. Just as my tenure as Casden Director was so greatly facilitated by my predecessor, founding Director Barry Glassner, now President of Lewis and Clark College, I hope that I have left Steve a good foundation upon which he can build and shape his own vision of the Casden Institute and its ongoing investigation of the Jewish role in American life.

I leave the last word for the two people who have been so essential to the success of my directorship of the Casden Institute. Marilyn J. Lundberg has been production editor of the *Annual Review* from my first volume and is also my closest academic supporter in so many ways. We have received consistent praise from our authors for the accurate presentations of their work. All credit for this goes to her. Lisa Ansell, Associate Director of the Casden Institute, has done everything anyone could ask to make the Casden Institute run as smoothly as it has while I have been its Director. Both Marilyn and Lisa have been the best collaborators I could ever hope to have. So it is to them both that I dedicate this volume.

Bruce Zuckerman, *Myron and Marian Casden Director*

Editorial Introduction

by Ari F. Sclar, Guest Editor

This volume focuses on a close examination of the relationship that American Jews have with sports. Granted, the stereotypical assumption is that Jews and sports are an oxymoronic pairing. Indeed, this relationship, and in fact, the very idea of a Jewish athlete, is one that remains distant from the broader consciousness of American Jewish life—even among many American Jews. As in the movie *Airplane!*, jokes about the absence of Jewish athleticism, often made by Jews themselves, are what most frequently comes to mind when the topic of Jews in sports is brought up. The stereotype of (generally male) Jewish physical inferiority has reinforced the belief that Jews focus on intellectual pursuits at the expense of physical activities. That is to say, a belief persists that they all tend to take after the biblical Jacob, favored by God, a momma's boy and one who kept to the tents, rather than his far more brawny and presumably more athletic brother Esau.

This assumption has its origins in the years after the Civil War, when white Anglo-Saxon Protestants became concerned that American men were not as rugged and masculine as their colonial and "frontier" forerunners. As Jewish immigration increased in the late nineteenth and early twentieth centuries, American Jews, anxious to emulate such nationalistic ideals, tried to overcome this stereotype by promoting Jewish participation in a masculine, American sporting culture that was generally open and amenable to their involvement. This was not done without some controversy and concern. While some Jews viewed sports as a symbol of modernity's threat to traditional Jewish culture and religion, others believed Jewish athleticism would serve as a positive development and would help produce full acceptance and integration into American society. Eventually, sports became one of many activities used to construct a modern American Jewish identity and, while acceptance was obviously not without struggle, Jews throughout the twentieth century (and now into the twenty-first) have participated and succeeded in the American sports culture as athletes, coaches, owners, managers and fans. As this volume intends to illustrate, the stereotype of the physical Jew may have drawn many Jews into the sporting world, but the broader connection between American Jews and sports goes well beyond such stereotypes.

Until recently, the study of Jews and sports was generally left to those with a narrowly focused interest in celebrating heroes—the "usual suspects" such as Sandy Koufax, Hank Greenberg, Sid Luckman and the like. The Bar Mitzvah gift books, celebrating famous Jews, always have left a little room for a few, select athletes, as has also been the case for various versions of the "Jewish Hall of Fame," web sites celebrating the accomplishment of Jews, and the occasional article in a Jewish magazine or newspaper about long celebrated or long forgotten heroes as well as contemporary athletes. Much of the celebratory history was dictated by an Americanization narrative that focused on the power of sports to overcome anti-Semitism and illustrate and facilitate the general tolerance of American society. The participation and success of Jewish athletes was seen as a means to dispel the stereotype of the weak Jew as a product of the large influx of eastern European Jewish immigrants and helped further advance Jewish acceptance in American society.

By the mid-twentieth century mark, as Jews moved into the suburbs, it was concluded that their socio-economic success meant that they no longer *needed* to play competitive sports in order to assimilate into American culture. Granted, the occasional Jewish star might emerge and attract national attention from Jews and non-Jews alike; but, as this narrative concluded, Jews had so successfully integrated into society that the stereotype no longer really applied. This narrative, while not necessarily incorrect, contains silences and absences that have inhibited our seeing a more complete picture of Jewish athleticism. Over the past twenty years, however, academics have begun to look more closely and seriously at this narrative and in doing so, have begun to look beyond the stereotypical viewpoint to see a more nuanced and subtle picture of Jews and their relationship to sports.

Not content merely to challenge the stereotype or celebrate the individual Jewish athlete, a number of scholars have worked to integrate the study of Jewish athleticism into the broader scholarship on American Jewish identity, community, and culture. This volume reflects this scholarly growth, as the discipline has moved beyond the need to overcome the idea that Jews are simply

"People of the Book," who never put the Book down to go out and compete in athletic events. Despite the continued belief that Jewish religious or cultural identity remains somehow distinct from the American idea of the "athlete," this collection of essays aims to demonstrate that American Jews have a close connection, and, indeed, have made highly significant contributions, to American sports, both on and off the field of play.

When Lisa Ansell, the Associate Director of the Casden Institute for the Study of the Jewish Role in America Life, first approached me and asked me to consider serving as guest editor for this volume, it was clear to me that she had her doubts whether the topic was sufficiently viable and expansive to merit an entire volume of studies. I assured her that, while Jews and their connection to sports unfortunately remain marginal topics in the minds of many academics and laypeople alike, it is nevertheless one that is attracting serious interest and active scholarly research. Our aim in this volume is to add substantively to this growing body of literature within the discipline, as it contains both articles that highlight the discovery of unknown history and those that offer fresh perspectives on seemingly well-established history.

The contributions in Volume 12 of the Casden *Annual Review* paint a broad—and at the same time highly detailed—picture of Jewish participation in sports and further examine how Jews viewed the business, religious, racial/ethnic, and identity questions associated with the athletic world. The complexity and diversity of the overall volume (with topics running a considerable gamut from tennis to lacrosse) underscore an essential concept: that Jewish athleticism cannot be defined by one athlete, sport, or context. Of course, this volume can hardly hope to cover all aspects of Jews and sports. Rather our aim is to examine and illustrate how research regarding American Jews and sports is moving in exciting and even surprising directions.

As with much of the literature on American Jews, the focus has remained fixed on how American men confronted anti-Semitism and the "90-pound weakling" stereotype, while unfortunately leaving women on the sidelines. For years, Linda Borish has worked to illustrate the important contributions of Jewish women to American sports and broader constructs of American Jewish identity, community, and culture. Examining a wide array of Jewish women in her many studies, Borish has challenged gendered understandings of what it meant to be an "athlete" and has helped sharpen the focus on women in sports. In this volume, she makes another important contribution—examining Jewish women in the early decades of the twentieth century in a sport not normally associated with Jews during that era: tennis. This former country club sport, which became popular with the wider sporting public during the interwar period, provided Jewish women with an opportunity to compete and be recognized on a national and international level. As Borish explains, this also allowed the Jewish press to celebrate women alongside their male counterparts in the American sports world. Although often condescendingly gendered by the press, female players achieved considerable success on the tennis courts and thus proved that Jewish women could define Jewish athleticism just as much as Jewish men have done so.

While Jewish women have rarely received the attention they deserve, Jews in ownership and/or management positions have received a bit more—but hardly sufficient—attention from scholars. Despite the stereotypical belief among many people that Jews are better suited to be owners rather than players, the extent of Jewish participation in management in a variety of sports prior to World War II remains relatively unexplored. Thus Rebecca Alpert's excellent examination of Negro League co-owner Effa Manley—a non-Jewish, biologically white female, who identified herself as African-American—shows how this formidable woman viewed Jewish owners in the Negro Leagues before the color bar was broken by Jackie Robinson in Major League Baseball. The often tense relationship between blacks and Jews, that is reflected in the original correspondence between Manley and her Jewish contemporaries uncovered by Alpert, spotlights issues of power, race, ethnicity, and finance—all of which still have a major impact on sports. As Alpert illustrates, Manley's attitude was complex and often ambivalent, depending on the situation, which in some ways mirrored African-American attitudes, and the attitude of Americans as a whole regarding the place of Jews in society. As Alpert notes, Jewish whiteness was implicitly recognized as acting as a wedge between Manley and the Jewish owners; and further highlights how their participation in the Negro Leagues reflected the extent to which Jews found the sporting world both open and closed to them. Jewish ownership of professional sports teams is now common, but in the early decades of the twentieth century, it proved more difficult for Jews to gain access to executive power in sports. Nonetheless, in relation to African-Americans, America's racial hierarchy tilted the power dynamic in the Jewish direction.

The secular demands of athletics have often proved to be an impediment for religious Jews, who desire to participate fully in the competitive culture of American sports. As Jeffrey Gurock has argued elsewhere, religious leaders often viewed sports as threatening to traditional Jewish values. But as he explains in this volume, overcoming traditional constraints to participate is not the end to the struggle. Orthodox Jews are limited in their ability to compete at the highest (or even middling) levels of competitive sports due more to religiously imposed internal restrictions than to external discrimination. This unique aspect of Jews in sports is one that other ethnic and racial groups have not generally confronted and adds a layer of complexity to the broader study of Jewish athleticism. As Gurock points out, this religious dynamic makes Yeshiva University basketball unique and interesting in a sporting world where all too frequently, competitive or commercial concerns predominate. Yeshiva competes, and has often competed well, but the school's struggles—as reflected in the trials and tribulations of its long-time basketball coach—reflect the difficulty for religious Jews, who despite having increasingly been accepted and celebrated in sports, remain at a disadvantage due to restrictions that secular Jews and non-Jews do not confront.

While many of the articles provide new information or capture previously unknown parts of Jews and sports, Joe Dorinson's provides a fresh perspective on a part of the sporting world that has long fascinated Jews: baseball. Using Martin Abramowitz's card collection as the point of departure for his study, Dorinson traces the long and vibrant history of Jews in baseball, from the earliest players and owners through Hall of Famers Hank Greenberg and Sandy Koufax and concludes with a glowing take on one of the most important figures in professional baseball history, Marvin Miller. Dorinson's narrative, which is adapted from an original oral presentation, illustrates the close relationship Jews have had since the beginning of the sport in a variety of ways. Yet, while Dorinson looks at America's national pastime, Neil Kramer examines a less well-known sport that has attracted Jewish players in recent years: lacrosse. Taking Israel's surprising success in the world lacrosse championships as his starting point, Kramer examines how lacrosse, like other sports, has helped facilitate Jewish integration into American society and how some hope that the sport will help better connect Jews with Israel. Lacrosse's appeal on an international scale may help construct the emerging American Jewish identity of the twenty-first century, which is shaping up to be quite different than the twentieth century.

I myself have contributed an article that considers many of the issues regarding Jews and sports noted above—in this case as seen in microcosm through the rise and fall of basketball at the 92nd Street Young Men's Hebrew Association (YMHA) in New York City. In its heyday, basketball was so closely identified with Jewish athletes that it was commonly called the "Jewish game," especially during the inter-World War period. Various conflicting views about how Jews should conduct themselves in sports led to a dilemma: the question was whether the Jewish version of basketball should focus on promoting the popularity of athletic stars or should instead pursue the selfless cooperation that were inherent in the ideals of the game? Due to an unsuccessful effort to resolve this dilemma at the YMHA and elsewhere, what was once the Jewish game became the Jewish game no more.

I want to thank Bruce Zuckerman, Myron and Marion Casden Director of the Casden Institute for the Study of the Jewish Role in American Life at the University of Southern California, and Lisa Ansell, Associate Director of the Casden Institute, for the opportunity to serve as the guest editor of this volume of the Casden *Annual Review*. The willingness and openness of both Bruce and Lisa to consider a volume on Jews and sports indicates the importance that the Casden Institute invests in expanding the broader understanding of the challenges and triumphs of American Jewry. As I worked closely with both of them, I saw their appreciation of the subject matter grow; and they, in some ways, represented the benefit the broader public would gain from such a volume. It also allowed me to work closely with a number of scholars whom I admire and respect and whose work both informs my own and challenges my understanding of the nuances and complexity of Jewish athleticism from a variety of perspectives.

Finally, I want to thank my wife, Rachael, for her support not only in this endeavor but throughout the years as I continue to examine the meanings associated with Jewish athleticism.

A Stack of Jewish Baseball Cards: Some Thoughts on Jews and the Roles They Have Played in the Major Leagues

by Joseph Dorinson

Jews love big-league baseball. That's all there is to it. Maybe this is the reason Martin Abramowitz's 2003 publication of his collection of 142 baseball cards featuring Jewish Major League Baseball (MLB) players sparked such widespread interest regarding the connection between Jews and baseball (and the history that lies behind this relationship). Still, if the Jews are the Chosen People, very few of them have been choice enough to make it in the Big Leagues even when you consider the additional twenty-eight Jewish players who have entered the majors between the release of Abramowitz's initial collection and the end of the 2013 season. As Boston *Globe* reporter Nathan Cobb observed at the time of Abramowitz's initial publication, Jews represent almost 3% of America's population but can only muster about .8% of this elite baseball fraternity (slightly improved in 2013 to a bit more than 1% of major league rosters) (Cobb). Of course, statistics do not get us behind the numbers. Maybe we dwell on the numbers because they are more easily measured than the intangibles that are really at the heart of this game so many of us love. Here, then are some numbers and accompanying thoughts about the Jewish men who have made their mark in and on MLB—both in and outside the white lines. Like Abramowitz's original 142 (now 170) baseball cards, they give us a chance to stay in touch with a less well-considered but no less well-loved part of American Jewish heritage.

First, some vital statistics, collected for us by Abramowitz along with his cards (and now updated with his help to reflect the numbers as of the end of the 2013 season): Over the years, Jewish batters have hit .265 on average as opposed to .262 for all the "others." Jewish pitchers also have enjoyed a slight edge over the rest of the field: a winning percentage of .504 versus .500. In 2003 Abramowitz noted the following regarding the Jews who played MLB: six pairs are brothers, three sons or grandsons of rabbis and ten have altered their names. In addition, through the 2013 season, Jewish baseball players have belted 2,887 home runs and knocked in 13,984 runs. Abramowitz may be gently chided in 2003 for understating the numbers of Sandy Koufax's no-hitters by one, attributing three, instead of four, to the Dodger hurler, who, during the five-year period from 1961 to 1966, established his credentials as one of the greatest pitchers ever (more on this below). During one conference at Cooperstown, Hall of Fame pitcher, "Rapid" Robert Feller, responding to a query from the audience, said that the greatest pitcher he ever saw was Sandy Koufax. No argument here. By the way, the other two no-hitters crafted by a Jewish pitcher were delivered by another southpaw, Ken Holtzman (Abramowitz 1–3; Feller).[1]

Our zealous statistician has also noted that Jewish pitchers fanned over eight percent more than they walked—11,761 versus 10,145. With evident pride, he made the further point that Giants' catcher, Hank Danning hit for the cycle (that is, a single, double, triple and homerun all in the same game)—only one of fourteen catchers ever to do so. He also identified the origins of his initial 142 subjects: 123 were born to two Jewish parents, six converted to Christianity, and thirteen had only one Jewish parent. A proud Bostonian, Abramowitz *kveled* with evident pride over the presence of nine Jews who wore Red Sox colors and three who played for the former "Beantown" Braves.

One glaring weakness of Jewish players, Abramowitz concedes, has been their lack of speed. They have stolen only 1449 bases. Brooklyn Dodger fans can attest to this painful fact in recalling the disaster of 1950: Wherein Cal Abrams, representing the winning run, was so slow around the bases that he was "gunned down" at the plate by the Phillies' notoriously weak-armed Richie Ashburn in the ninth inning of the deciding final game of the season, thereby blowing the League Championship and losing the Pennant that is its emblem. Many years later, in an event sponsored by the Brooklyn Historical Society, the late Dodger outfielder *insisted* that he was actually a pretty fast runner. Many in the audience, including this writer, groaned in disbelief.

Literary critic Eric Solomon posits several salient reasons for the love connection between Jews and baseball. First, he writes, baseball provided "a superb avenue for acculturation." Evidence of this assertion can be found in the writings of Abe Cahan. In his novel, *Yekl* (1896), the renowned Yiddish journalist equated baseball with Americanization. Second, the national pastime appealed to Jewish intellect due to its penchant for dialectics and documentation. Third, baseball sparked outstanding literature, privileging heads (the *Yiddishe kep*, to put this in the Jewish vernacular) over hands. Fourth, this city-game lured urban youngsters from out of their tenement enclaves in the ghettos. After all, what could be more urban about the Jewish experience than the transition from the *shtetl* to Gotham? Finally, baseball culture engaged Jewish sensibilities. As Eric Solomon noted:

> ... the national game rich in folklore, deep in mythology, full of anecdote in the Sholem Aleichem mode, cabbalistic in numerology, quasi-religious in gods, creative in language ... denying time's rules while emphasizing the conflict between youth and age—mythic, historical, spiritual, simple and complex. Harsh and beautiful, real and fictional ... baseball, in simple, is America. (Solomon 77–78)

Baseball has unleashed vast stores of Jewish creativity. Witness the novels of Bernard Malamud, Philip Roth, Mark Harris, Jerome Charyn, Jay Neugeboren, and Eric Greenberg, the print journalism of Roger Kahn, Dick Young, Stan Isaacs, Maury Allen, Lester Rodney, and Bob Lipsyte, the broadcast journalism of Mel Allen (*ne* Israel), Marty Glickman, Al Michaels, Charlie Steiner, Warner Wolf, and Chris Berman to name just a few of the best. And, *sui generis*, there is also that hyperbolic wordsmith and solipsistic narcissist, Howard Cosell, who in many respects epitomized the best (and worst) with regard to the Jewish love of sports. Moreover, renowned public relations executive Marty Appel pointed out that the Jewish-baseball connection has always flourished in his field of wish-fulfillment, i.e., dreams under the aegis of creative Jews like Bob Fishel (and, I submit for the record, the genial Mr. Appel as well). With regard to the music-baseball connection, Jews also have excelled. Most notably, Albert Von Tilzer composed that all-time favorite, "Take Me Out to the Ballgame" (1908) and Paul Simon penned a lament for a vanishing hero in the line, "Where Have You, Gone, Joe DiMaggio?" that became a kind of eulogy for the fading twentieth century (Solomon 76–77; Riess, "From Pike to Green" 134–35).[2]

Baseball's first Jewish professional (the first baseball card in our collection, as it were) was Lipman Pike, who earned $20 weekly as a second baseman (historian Peter Bjarkman placed him at third) for the Philadelphia Athletics in 1866. He hit .300 plus for ten seasons. According to Bjarkman and Roger Abrams, on July 16, 1866, Pike slugged six home runs in a single game—five in succession. Not only did Pike earn the distinction of being the first Jewish professional baseball player, he also became the game's first slugger, bearing the appropriate moniker of the "Iron Batter" (Abrams 148–59; Bjarkman 307). In addition to his exploits on the "field of dreams," he managed baseball for three years after he retired as an active player.

Historian Steven Riess declared that Jews gravitated to the business side of baseball, citing John M. Brunswick as the first such entrepreneur. [*Eds. Note*: See the article by Rebecca Alpert also in this volume.] These businessmen, primarily German-Jewish in origin, sought social acceptance as well as private gain through their baseball investments. Present at the creation were such Jewish owners as Nathan Andersen, Aaron Stern, Louis Kramer, and Julius Fleischmann. Another, Andrew Freedman, used his Tammany Hall connections to gain a controlling interest in the New York Giants from 1895 to 1902. Apparently, he had a well-earned reputation as a loutish owner, who lacked both diplomatic skills and the social graces. Roger Abrams scornfully described him as "arrogant, overbearing, and insufferable," and compared him with a more contemporary *bête noire*, George Steinbrenner of Yankee fame, because he fired sixteen managers in eight years (Abrams 159). Still, Freedman took no guff with regard to his Jewishness. He once punched a *New York Times* reporter in the nose and pulled his team off the field in response to anti-Semitic remarks of a former player, James "Ducky" Holmes. He also tried to create a J. P. Morgan-like trust to control the game (Riess, "From Pike to Green" 117–19). Forced from the helm, he arranged transfer of ownership to another Tammany favorite, Charles Stoneham, later of Giants' fame. A more benign brand of Jewish ownership could be found in Pittsburgh under the aegis of Barney Dreyfuss, in Boston under Emil Fuchs, and more recently in Milwaukee under Bud Selig before he became MLB commissioner.

Eastern European Jews might have tended to gravitate to a more street-oriented sport—basketball. [*Eds. Note*: See also the article by Ari Sclar also in this volume.] Baseball required more green space than was generally available in urban ghettoes. And truth be told, Jewish parents mostly preferred that their offspring focused on work, study, and practicing the piano rather than playing sports. "To the pious people of the Ghetto," comedian Eddie Cantor asserted, "a baseball player was the king of the loafers" (Riess, "Baseball and Ethnicity" 89). Nevertheless, many youths found baseball congenial as spectators as well as participants. Settlement houses encouraged sports among the immigrant children. Abe Cahan's Yiddish daily, *Der Forvertz* (*The Forward*) characterized the rules of the game as a means to a desirable end—assimilation into mainstream

America. In his previously mentioned novel, *Yekl*, Cahan used baseball to illustrate the tensions within society. His protagonist, Yekl, loved baseball and boxing. For him, sports provided acceptance just as it conferred identity (Levine 87–88). After all, baseball represented a "secular nationalistic church" that historian Peter Levine has argued, "helped mitigate conflict between generations" (98). Already assimilated, affluent German-American Jews feared that their "co-religionists" from Eastern Europe posed a threat because they were "often charged with lack of physical courage and repugnance to physical work." Therefore, anxious American Jews promoted the creation of settlement houses to craft a counter-image. Beginning in 1889, one of many agencies on the Lower East Side of Manhattan, the Educational Alliance, attempted to reverse common perceptions through athletic training. "Let a young man develop his body, and he will neither shrink from imaginary danger nor shirk manual labor which falls to his lot" (*Official Souvenir Book* 19–23).

First among equals in athletic training, baseball proved enormously successful as an agent for acculturation. On the other hand, it also created something of a crisis for Jews following the infamous 1919 World Series between the Chicago White Sox and the Cincinnati Reds. The "fix" involved two prominent Jewish gamblers, Arnold "Whitey" Rothstein and former featherweight boxing champ, Abe Attell; and the resulting scandal fueled anti-Semitic sentiment. Henry Ford's *Dearborn Independent* spread the most vicious canards whose intention was to do their utmost to slander and disparage the Jewish people. Two articles, which appeared in September 1921, focused on Rothstein and Attell as "Jewish dupes" who conned Gentile "boobs." Ford warned against a Jewish conspiracy to corrupt baseball and other "Anglo-Saxon institutions" (Nathan 96–98).

Reacting to pervasive anti-Semitism, some Jewish ballplayers changed their names. *New York Times* writer, Ira Berkow, author of the definitive book about Hank Greenberg, identified ten players who changed their names for "business" reasons. He cited a number of Cohens who "morphed" into Corey, a White Sox pitcher, Ewing, a Cardinal shortstop, Bohne, an infielder with several teams, Kane, a Phillies pitcher, and Cooney, a Yankee third baseman (Berkow 2). They could run, as Joe Louis observed with regard to his opponent, non-Jewish Billy Conn, but they could not hide. This became ever clearer with the rise of Germany's malevolent leader, Adolf Hitler, who would do all within his power to preclude this escape by way of assimilation as he rose to power on the wings of "Jew-phobia."

The Great Depression both weakened the fabric of society and curtailed intercultural communication. Unhappy days were here again, and American

Jewry suffered the slings and arrows of outrageous defamation. Historian Leonard Dinnerstein argued that "anti-Semitic displays did not increase with the onset of the Great Depression" (Dinnerstein 105). From 1929 to 1933, he declared, Jews were spared the bigots' bromides. Be that as it may, after the election of Franklin D. Roosevelt and Hitler's ascent, combined with the deepening economic woes of 1933, American Jews experienced violent physical assaults, especially in New York City and Boston. Hitler's vicious attacks struck a responsive chord with many Americans, who needed a scapegoat to explain their misery. Sinclair Lewis's fictional "It" (of his 1935 satirical, political novel, *It Can't Happen Here*) could—and, indeed, did— happen here. As has been well studied and documented, quotas prevented Jewish entry into medical schools and other institutions of learning; restrictive covenants barred Jews from residential areas; and large law firms that did not actually bar Jews from employment marginalized them. Many adherents of Father Charles E. Coughlin and Gerald L. K. Smith linked Jews with either heartless capitalism or zealous communism—indifferent to the logical contradictions in such claims. Virulent attacks were particularly popularized by the "radio priest" Coughlin, who shamelessly plagiarized propagandist Joseph Goebbels and his minions (Bird 55–56; Brinkley 266).

Nevertheless, in these same 1930s, baseball witnessed the entry into the Major Leagues of more Jewish ballplayers than ever before: twenty-five (exceeded only during the 1940s). These newcomers proved physically tough as well as intellectually astute. Buddy Myer, an outstanding Washington Senator shortstop and subsequent second baseman, enjoyed a stellar seventeen-year career, during which he batted .303. In 1935, he captured the American League batting crown with a robust .349 average. His most remembered "hit," however, probably occurred in 1933 when Yankee bigot Ben Chapman attempted to maim Myer in the course of breaking up a double-play. Chapman, who would later try to run Jackie Robinson out of baseball, got it right in the *punim* (the Jewish moniker for "mug") in swift retaliation. Although the Yankees beat the Senators 16 to 0, the fight between Myer and Chapman stole the headlines (Levine 126; Horwitz and Horwitz 123–25).

Princeton graduate and premier catcher, Moe Berg, reputedly knew twelve languages and, as the old joke goes, hit .200 in all of them. He also "doubled" in a most unorthodox manner—as an OSS spy for his country during World War II (Dawidoff). However, neither the competent Myer nor the intellectual Berg could match Hank Greenberg in mass appeal. Without a doubt, the national pastime produced an exemplary role-model in Henry Louis

Greenberg, a strong Jew who fought back. The impact of this American Jewish hero has been chronicled extensively, but his stature, like the Passover story, invites periodic retelling. In an age of increasing anti-Semitism, this Bronx slugger in a Detroit Tiger uniform served as both a beacon of light and a pillar of strength. As we have already noted, Detroit's atmosphere was polluted by the fulminations of radio priest, Father Coughlin and the anti-Semitic tirades of auto tycoon Henry Ford. As MVP in 1935 and again in 1940, at two different positions, Greenberg challenged the stereotype of the spineless Jew. After a distinguished military record in World War II, he returned home in 1945, to become an icon for all Americans (Dorinson 66–82; Simons 83–102).

It is important to note, too, that "Hammerin' Hank" took a role in advancing the cause of racial integration. For example, in 1947, as a member of the Pirates, he was the first Dodger-opponent to openly encourage and support Jackie Robinson. Recalling his own struggle with bigotry, the veteran Jewish slugger exhorted the rookie Robinson to "Stick in there. You're doing fine. Keep your chin up." After an accidental collision at first base, in which the lumbering Hank and the nimble Jackie became entangled, reporters, eager to stir up controversy, tried to incite the Dodger rookie in order to get some headline-making trash-talk about Greenberg out of him. But Robinson disappointed them by replying: "Class tells. It sticks out all over Mr. Greenberg" (Rampersad 177; Tygiel 192; Norwood and Blackman 121–31).

The Jewish fan-base ran especially especially deep in Brooklyn, and they revered Jackie Robinson. In a book that I co-edited with Joram Warmund, *Jackie Robinson: Race, Sport, and the American Dream*, there is section that we called "Fans' Remembrances," wherein, among others, Robert Gruber, Peter Williams, Ivan Hametz, Peter Levine, and Henry Foner evoked their personal recollections of the unconquerable trailblazer. Each contributor conveyed in highly personal terms the significance of Robinson's advent. For Jews especially, Jackie epitomized the hopes as well as the dreams of a truly pluralistic America. Perhaps Foner said it best when, as the youngest of four famous brothers, he began *die fir kashes* ("the four questions") on the first Passover night in 1947. "Why is this night different from all others?" Usurping the role of patriarch, young Henry answered his own question in a novel way: "Today, the first black American player entered the major leagues" (Foner 71; others in Dorinson and Warmund 43–69).

Jewish sportswriters Lester Rodney and Bill Mardo battled bigotry from the press box. As sports editor and writer, respectively, for the *Daily Worker*, a communist paper, Rodney and Mardo waged a relentless campaign against

Jim Crow baseball. Jules Tygiel has credited Rodney and his cadres with "forcing the issue before the American public . . ." and in conjunction with the black press and a small coterie of white sportswriters, many of them Jewish, "helped to alleviate the apathy that nourished baseball segregation" (Tygiel 36–37; Rampersad 120). In Irwin Silber's memoir, *Press Box Red*, we learn how Rodney launched his crusade against segregation in 1936. Graciously, he paid homage to other writers, namely, Heywood Broun, Ted Benson, and surprisingly, the arch-conservative journalist and gadfly Westbrook Pegler for their efforts in this righteous cause. He also mentioned Joe DiMaggio favorably for stating in 1937 that the most difficult pitcher for him to hit was Leroy "Satchel" Paige (Silber 63–64). Oddly, Rodney mentioned Hank Greenberg only once in his book. Nevertheless, in conversations with this writer, he expressed deep admiration for the Jewish slugger, who interrupted a sensational baseball career to fight fascism abroad.

Returning to the game inside the white lines, Hank Greenberg passed the baton, so to speak, to Cleveland Indians all-star Al Rosen, whose Hall of Fame potential was cut short by injury. In his first full season as a major leaguer in 1950, he hit a league leading 37 home runs. The next year, "Flip" Rosen, while playing in all 154 games, slugged four grand slam home runs. In 1953, he was an unprecedented unanimous choice for American League MVP with a dazzling .336 batting average, forty-three homers, and 145 RBIs, just missing the coveted batting triple-crown by a thousandth of a point. Perhaps his finest hour came in the 1954 All-Star game, in which he banged out two homers and collected five RBIs. Rosen, who was active in Jewish charities and an excellent boxer, was never reluctant to defend the Jewish faith with his fists. Once a White Sox opponent called him a "Jew bastard." Sox pitcher Saul Rogovin, also Jewish, remembered an angry Rosen striding belligerently to the dugout and challenging the "son of a bitch" to a fight. Living up to the label with which Rosen had branded him, the mongrel froze in silence. During a ten-year career, Rosen averaged .285 and totaled 192 home runs. He followed this with a successful career in finance, but his love for baseball brought him back to the executive suite as either president or general manager successively of the Yankees, Astros, and Giants. To those—like the stone-faced journalist and TV impresario Ed Sullivan, who questioned how true he was to his Jewish identity, Al Rosen could proudly claim that he never played on Yom Kippur (Riess, "From Pike to Green" 130; Levine 128; Horvitz and Horvitz 145–46).

As we examine our collection of 170 Jews in MLB, Sandy Koufax clearly merits special mention for his extraordinary exploits as the Jewish "main man" on the mound. However, as Jane Leavy revealed in her book, the Dodger great encountered prejudice throughout his rise to fame. Despite considerable progress brought about by Jackie Robinson's breakthrough, to which prominent Jewish figures contributed, the virus of bigotry remained virulent. Like Greenberg and Rosen before him, Koufax was not particularly religious. Nevertheless, he felt compelled to identify with his Jewishness, especially on the holiest of days. Most famously, Koufax refused to pitch a World Series game on Yom Kippur in 1965. Mets owner Fred Wilpon, a friend since high school, insisted that Koufax was deeply Jewish primarily because of his New York background (Leavy 182). The second Jewish player (the first was Hank Greenberg) to enter Cooperstown's Hall of Fame, Koufax's spectacular career was also shortened by injury. From 1961 to 1966, he was widely considered the best pitcher in baseball. In that period, Sandy hurled four no-hitters, including a perfect game against the Cubs on September 9, 1965. In 1963, he pitched eleven shutouts. During his illustrious though injury-shortened career, Koufax earned three CyYoung awards, one MVP, amassed 165 wins and a career 2.76 ERA. Twice, the Brooklyn-born lefthander struck out 18 batters in a single game. He led the light-hitting Dodgers to three Word Series championships in four attempts with an astonishing .095 post-season ERA. Koufax won the strikeout title four times, once with a record 382 Ks. Whether the sensational southpaw encountered his quota of anti-Semitism is still a moot subject. Steven Riess categorized this once virulent outbreak as a minimum threat while, as indicated earlier, Leavy, in a more recent study, documented its persistence (Leavy 71–73, 176–83; Riess, "From Pike to Green" 131).

In his seminal study, Riess illustrated that the number of Jewish participants in MLB fluctuated from decade to decade. He identified, for example, five in the 1900s, eleven in the 1910s, twenty-three in the 1960s, nineteen in the 1970s, and ten in the 1980s ("From Pike to Green" 122, 131).[3] Careers open to talent beckoned elsewhere. Still, the recently retired Shawn Green continued the tradition begun by Lipman Pike. Awarded a scholarship to Stanford University, Green made it to the "Bigs" in 1993 and soon blossomed into a slugging star with the Toronto Blue Jays. In his first full year in the American League, Shawn hit .288 with thirty-one doubles and fifteen home runs. 1999 proved to be Green's best year in Toronto, when he hit .309, slugged forty-two home runs, and knocked in 123 runs. Giving the lie to the "slow Jew" stereotype, Shawn stole twenty bases in twenty-seven attempts and scored 134 runs. Then, after several outstanding seasons with his bat, glove, and feet, Green returned to his native grounds in California as part of a trade for Raul Mondesi with the LA Dodgers. In moving to Los Angeles, Shawn tripled his annual salary, zooming from $3,125,000 to $9,416,667. Green's best statistical year in LA was in 2001, when he blasted forty-nine home runs, recorded 124 RBIs, sported a .297 batting average and stole twenty bases in twenty-four attempts ("Shawn Green" 1–4). Green's singular assault on Milwaukee pitching in May 2002 was one for the record books. On that memorable day, he hammered out four home runs, a double and a single, scored six runs, and had seven RBIs in a single game (Chass)!

We, who are less gifted, persevere as dreamers, spectators, and overall *mayvns* by remembering such athletic feats. Eric Solomon concluded his brilliant essay with an apposite reference to William Carlos Williams' "The Crowd at the Ball Game," in which New Jersey's preeminent poet-physician praised the Jew in the crowd because:

> The Jew gets it straight—it
> is deadly, terrifying—
>
> It is the Inquisition, the
> Revolution
>
> It is beauty itself . . . (Solomon 98)

In her brilliantly crafted book, Leavy, citing Fred Wilpon, observed astutely that the Koufax-Don Drysdale holdout in 1965 constituted the legendary southpaw's finest hour off the field—"the most underestimated event in Koufax's career" (Leavy 201). By bargaining collectively for the first time, Koufax and Drysdale (the twin towers of Dodger pitching power) ignited a revolution. Their stand in turn cleared the way for the heaviest Jewish hitter in the annals of American baseball. Granted, he never stood in physically at the plate, but Major League Baseball Players Association (MLBPA) leader Marvin Miller should be added as an honorary 171st to the other 170 MLB Jews for all he did by going to bat for all the Major League players. Indeed, while the two dominant pitchers proved vital to the eventual emergence of free agency, Miller brought a social conscience, rooted in trade union culture, grounded in prophetic tradition, and leavened with core values. Miller remembered that his father worked in lower Manhattan dispensing *tsedaka* (alms) and wisdom in Chinese, English, and Yiddish (Miller, *A Whole Different Ball Game* 13; Miller, Personal Interview 1–3). *The Sporting News* listed Miller as Number Five among the top one hundred most powerful people in twentieth century American sports. In 1994, *Sports Illustrated* ranked Miller as Number Seven in the top forty most influential figures in sports, placing him ahead of Wayne Gretsky, Arnold Palmer, Larry Bird, and Pete Rozelle. Walter Lanier "Red" Barber, the premier play-by-play announcer and commentator for the Dodgers and mentor to his illustrious successor, Vin Scully, identified Marvin Miller, along with Babe Ruth and Jackie Robinson, as one of the three most important men in baseball (Barra 1–3; "Marvin Miller"). Of this trinity, only Miller has remained inexplicably excluded from the Hall of Fame even though his leadership of the Players' Union from 1966 to 1982, brought spectacular progress that culminated in a breakthrough in 1984. His efforts allowed the "diamond-workers" to gain full dignity, contractual freedom, monetary rewards, and occupational safety.

Born in the Bronx, Miller grew up in Brooklyn. His mother Gertrude taught public school while his father, Abraham, was a salesman in Manhattan. Marvin graduated from Brooklyn's James Madison High School, where he will be inducted into the school's hall of fame as of October 2014 and from which he graduated in 1932. Marvin started his college career at Miami of Ohio but finished at NYU in 1936, the same year he met his future wife, Theresa Morgenstern. They were married for seventy years before she died in 2009, and Miller survived her by three more years. Marvin's work resumé included a stint of government service during World War II, and work with the Machinists' Union, the United Auto Workers, and the Steelworkers Union from 1950 to 1964 as staff-economist, chief-economist, advisor, and assistant to Union President David McDonald (Miller, *A Whole Different Ballgame* 11–32).

In 1966, ace pitchers as well as energetic player-union leaders, Robin Roberts and Jim Bunning urged Marvin Miller to head their fledgling union after Judge Robert Cannon (a management representative) spurned their collective-bargaining offer. Through careful planning coupled with labor savvy, Miller won over dissidents and crafted a united front, resulting in a progression of victories that included raises in both minimum wage and average salary, improvements in safety standards, better fringe benefits, and increased pension allotments.

As Miller recalled in his illuminating memoir, his first major decision was to nix Richard Nixon as the union's legal counsel (Miller, *A Whole Different Ballgame* 33, 82–83). Then he took on the Topps Chewing Gum Co., which was paying a mere $125 per player for those highly valuable memorabilia, that have served as the point of departure for these musings on Jews in MLB—namely, baseball cards. Applying muscle, Miller managed to wrest huge residuals from Topps for the hitherto exploited players. By the end of 1966, the increasingly confident Miller had secured an agreement, which brought $4.1 million in annual funds (up from $1.5 million) for the players' retirement plan. This Basic Agreement also doubled prior monthly disability and pension payments. Miller accepted a flat sum, rather than a percentage, from All-Star and World Series proceeds. Through it all, Miller listened, learned, and educated. Slowly, he convinced the players that, rather than being expendable chattel, they were of fundamental importance to the baseball scene and deserved appropriate compensation.

Inviting a list of grievances (*cahiers*), Miller heard about the lack of safety in Cincinnati's Crosley Field, the fleabag hotels on the road, the doubleheaders after night games, and even the need for more outlets for hair-dryers. Advising the "angries" to "cool" it, Miller morphed into a Great Educator as well as Great Emancipator. He demanded—and received—data on salaries. Then he acted in concert with union members, who started their movement with a $344 annual dues payment. Dodger owner Walter O'Malley (according to writer Pete Hamill) reputedly bellowed: "Tell that Jewish boy to get back to Brooklyn" (Helyer 39).

The first comprehensive Basic Agreement, signed in February 1968, raised minimum salaries from $6,000 to $10,000 and directed the arbitration of grievances to the Commissioner. When the latter, William "Spike" Eckert, sided with the players on one issue, he was promptly fired, paving the way for Bowie Kuhn to take charge. Kuhn persuaded the owners to compromise, and a strike was averted in 1969. That same year, an irate Curt Flood refused to be traded from the Cardinals to the Phillies. Kuhn tried to maintain the status quo, and so, with the full support of Miller and the MLBPA, Flood sued. Initiated in 1970, Flood's litigation culminated in a 1972 decision in which the Supreme Court ruled against him, 5 to 3.

Nevertheless, the artful Miller secured a second Basic Agreement from baseball's management, which raised minimum salaries in graduated steps: to $12,000 in 1972 and then to $15,000 in 1975. It also reduced the maximum pay cut in a single year from 30% to 20%. Finally the Basic Agreement provided for impartial arbitration of grievances, thereby bypassing the Commissioner's office. When the owners attempted to block additional union progress, the players called a general strike, their first ever, on April 1, 1972. They were not bluffing. The strike lasted for thirteen days and cost eighty-six games. At that point, the owners capitulated. The pension payments were pegged to inflation and rose accordingly.

March 1973 produced another Basic Agreement containing impressive gains. Minimum salaries rose to $16,000. The "Flood Rule" led to a ten-year option (five with the same club) that empowered the veteran players to reject trades. Of equal importance, the Agreement provided for impartial salary arbitration. In 1975, Miller chalked up additional victories by freeing Jim "Catfish" Hunter from the clutches of Oakland owner Charles Finley because he had failed to comply with contractual obligations. Realizing that clause 10B of the Uniform Players Contract provided a wedge that would lead toward free agency, Miller launched an assault on the reserve clause with Andy Messersmith and Dave McNally as frontline litigants. Free agency was upheld initially by a three-person arbitration panel and subsequently reaffirmed by the Supreme Court. The players, to echo Dr. King, were "free at last." Since 1922, baseball players had been yoked to a team for life via a "reserve clause," because of a long-ago judicial decision handed down by Justice Oliver Wendell Holmes, no less. In a 7–2 verdict, Holmes had spoken for the majority, when he ruled that baseball was a sport, not a business thereby "starting"—in Miller's trenchant words—"a whitewash of the baseball monopoly" (Miller, *A Whole Different Ballgame* 42). Finally, thanks to Miller's efforts this infamous landmark Holmes decision of 1922 was overturned.

The "Lords of Baseball," in John Helyard's descriptive phrase, tried to turn back the clock by perpetrating a lockout in 1976 and seeking compensation for free agents in 1981, only to be defeated again by player solidarity that culminated in a strike initiated on June 12, 1981. It lasted fifty days with a loss of 713 games. A compromise settlement permitted teams to protect twenty-four players and a gain of one player in the amateur draft for a player lost to another club. Miller had ample cause to take pride in these achievements (Roberts and Olsen 136–37, 153–56).[4] All that remains is for him to gain entry into Baseball's Valhalla in Cooperstown. The "Lords" evidently underestimated Marvin Miller whose calm demeanor "belied a ferociously tenacious personality" (Roberts and Olsen 136). Economist Andrew Goodman correctly observed that Miller's other contributions, less familiar to baseball aficionados, led to greater safety. These largely ignored innovations that he brought to MLB included "improved scheduling and padded outfield walls, better-defined warning tracks, and safer locker rooms" (Goodman 3). Moreover, tennis great Arthur Ashe asserted that Marvin Miller had contributed "more for the welfare of black athletes than anyone else" (Barra 1).

As educator as well as liberator, the late Marvin Miller had much to teach us, if only we had listened and learned. Upon receiving the John Commerford award from the New York Labor History Association, actor and trade union leader Theodore Bikel offered the following eloquent translation:

> Now awake, the end's in sight
> See your power, feel your might
> Were it not for your strong hand
> Not a wheel would turn in the all the
> land. (*Work History News* 4)

Miller brought baseball and its workmen out of the wilderness into full dignity as well as ample compensation: Freedom from indentured servitude to realization of the American Dream.

One hundred and seventy might not seem a very large set of baseball cards (even when you add an extra honorary card for Marvin Miller), when stacked up against all the thousands of other MLB cards and the personalities, statistics, heroics, wins, loses, championships, also-rans and general ups and downs that they represent. It's a select, even an unlikely group that, if not culled from and separated out of the bigger pile, might not be very noticeable at all. Still, Jews have come a long way since Lipman Pike first strode to the plate, both on the field and off. Abramowitz the collector and chronicler, has had good reason to draw this small group to our collective attention. Granted, the 170 Jews who have played The Game and hopefully those who will add to their numbers in the future are not usually the biggest or the brightest lights to shine in our national ballparks. Nonetheless, they call attention to a unique nexus between an ethnic and an athletic culture that in its own peculiar way is as American as peanuts and crackerjacks.

Notes

1. Also see Benson 1–4. Bob Feller's appraisal of Sandy Koufax was articulated at the 16th Annual Cooperstown Symposium on Baseball & American Culture in an interview by Edwin L. Plowman. We wish to thank Mr. Abramowitz, who has, as noted, updated the statistics to reflect, to the extent possible, the current numbers as of the close of the 2013 season (personal communication).
2. Marty Appel shared his insights with this author in an email exchange, 25 June 2004.
3. Bjarkman (343) notes that Jewish participation peaked with twenty-seven in the 1940s. Bjarkman's overall data may be suspect; he erroneously identifies Ed Reulbach and Rod Carew as Jewish.
4. Roberts and Olson provide an excellent and succinct summary of Marvin Miller's achievements.

Works Cited

Abramowitz, Martin. "American Jews in America's Game: The Making of a Card Set." *Jewish Major Leaguers: Baseball Cards*. New York: American Historical Society, 2003.

Abrams, Roger. *The First World Series and the Baseball Fanatics of 2003*. Boston: Northeastern, 2003.

Appel, Marty. E-Mail exchange. 25 June 2004.

Baldassaro, Lawrence, and Richard Johnson, eds. *The American Game: Baseball and Ethnicity*. Carbondale, IL: Illinois, 2002.

Barra, Allen. "Marvin Miller: Hall of Famer." *Salon.com News*, 3 Jan. 2001. 19 Aug. 2014 <http://www.salon.com/2001/01/03/miller_15/>.

Benson, Mark. "A Jewish Baseball Card Series." *JTA*, 11 Nov. 2002. 19 Aug. 2014 <http://www.jta.org/2002/11/11/life-religion/features/a-jewish-baseball-cards-series>.

Berkow, Ira. "In David's Footsteps: Despite Obstacles Jews Have Made History in Nearly Every Sport." *Forward*, 6 Feb. 2004. 19 Aug. 2014 <http://forward.com/articles/6264/in-david-s-footsteps/>.

Bird, Caroline. *The Invisible Scar*. New York: David McKay, 1966.

Bjarkman, Peter. "Six Pointed Diamonds and the Ultimate Shicksa: Baseball and the American Jewish Immigrant Experience." *Cooperstown Symposium on Baseball and the American Culture*. Ed. Alvin L. Hall. Westport, CT: Meckler, 1991.

Brinkley, Alan. *Voices of Protest: Huey Long, Father Coughlin and the Great Depression*. New York: Random House Vintage, 1983.

Chass, Murray. "Dodgers and Reds Sit on Opposite Ends of Season's Seesaw." *New York Times* 30 May 2004: SP 2.

Cobb, Nathan. "Tribute Is in the Cards for Jewish Ballplayers." *Boston Globe* 23 Oct. 2003: D1, D5.

Dawidoff, N. *The Catcher Was a Spy: The Mysterious Life of Moe Berg*. New York: Vintage, 1994.

Dinnerstein, Leonard. *Anti-semitism in America*. New York: Oxford Univ., 1984.

Dorinson, Joseph. "Baseball Ethnic Heroes: Hank Greenberg and Joe DiMaggio." *The Cooperstown Symposium on Baseball and the American Culture 2001*. Ed. William M. Simons and Alvin L. Hall. Jefferson, NC: McFarland, 2002. 66–82.

Dorinson, Joseph, and Joram Warmand, eds. *Jackie Robinson: Race, Sports and the American Dream*. Armonk, NY: Sharpe, 1999.

Eisen, George, and David K. Wiggins, eds. *Ethnicity and Sport in North America and Culture*. Westport, CT: Praeger, 1994.

Feller, Bob. Interview with Edward L. Plowman. 16th Annual Symposium on Baseball and the American Culture. 3 June 2004.

Foner, Henry. "Mah Nishtanah," *Jackie Robinson: Race, Sports, and the American Dream*. Ed. Joseph Dorinson and Joram Warmund. Armonk, NY: Sharpe, 1999.

Goodman, Andrew. "Sportslaw History: The Role of Marvin Miller." *Sportslaw news. com*. <http://www.sportslawnews.com/archive/history/MarvinMiller.htm>.

Helyar, John. *Lords of the Realm: the Real History of Baseball*. New York: Ballantine, 1994.

Horwitz, Peter S., and Joachim Horwitz. *The Big Book of Jewish Baseball*. New York: SPI Books, 2001.

Leavy, Jane. *Sandy Koufax: A Lefty's Legacy*. New York: Harper Collins, 2002.

Levine, Peter. *Ellis Island to Ebbets Field: Sport and the American Jewish Experience*. New York: Oxford Univ., 1992.

Lewis, Sinclair. *It Can't Happen Here*. New York: Doubleday, 1935.

Miller, Marvin. *A Whole Different Ballgame: The Sport and Business of Baseball*. New York: Birch Lane, 1991.

———. Personal Interview. *Marvin Miller Papers*. Ed. Gail Malgren. Wagner Archives. Box Five, Folder 11. NYU Tamiment Library.

"Marvin Miller." *Jews in Sports*. 19 Aug. 2014 <http://www.jewsinsports.org>.

Nathan, David A. "Anti-Semitism and the Black Sox Scandal." *Nine* 4 (Fall 1995): 94–100.

Norwood, Stephen, and Harold Blackman. "Going to Bat for Jackie Robinson: The Jewish Role in Breaking the Color Line." *Journal of Sports History* 26 (Spring 1999): 121–31.

Official Souvenir Book of the Fair: In Aid of the Educational Alliance and the Hebrew Technical Institute, 1895.

Rampersad, Arnold. *Jackie Robinson: A Biography*. New York: Knopf, 1997.

Riess, Stephen A. "Baseball and Ethnicity." *Baseball As America: Seeing Ourselves Through Our National Pastime*. Washington, DC: National Geographic and National Baseball Hall of Fame and Museum, 2002.

———. "From Pike to Green with Greenberg in Between: Jewish Americans and the American Immigrant Experience." *The American Game: Baseball and Ethnicity*. Ed. Lawrence Baldassaro and Richard A. Johnson. Carbondale, IL: Southern Illinois Univ., 2002.

Roberts, Randy, and James Olson. *Winning Is the Only Thing: Sports in America Since 1945*. Baltimore: Johns Hopkins, 1989.

Rubin, Ruth. *Voice of a People: The Story of Yiddish Folksong*. New York: McGraw-Hill, 1973.

"Shawn Green." *Baseball-Reference.com*. 19 Aug. 2014 <http://www.baseball-reference.com/players/g/greensh01.shtml?redir>.

Silber, Irwin. *Press Box Red: The Story of Lester Rodney, the Communist Who Helped Break the Color Line in American Sports*. Philadelphia: Temple, 2003.

Simon, Paul, composer. "Mrs. Robinson." Columbia, 1968.

Simons, William M. "Searching for Hank Greenberg: Aviva Kempner's Mythic Hero and Our Fathers." *The Cooperstown Symposium on Baseball and the American Culture 2001 and 2002*. Ed. William M. Simons and Alvin L. Hall. Jefferson, NC: McFarland, 2002, 2003. 83–102.

Simons, William M., and Alvin L. Hall eds. *The Cooperstown Symposium on Baseball and the American Culture 2001 and 2002*. Jefferson, NC: McFarland, 2002, 2003.

Solomon, Eric. "Jews and Baseball: A Cultural Love Story." *Ethnicity and Sport in North American History and Culture*. Ed. George Eisen and David K. Wiggins. Westport, CT: Praeger, 1994.

Tygiel, Jules. *Baseball's Great Experiment: Jackie Robinson and His Legacy*. New York: Random House Vintage, 1984.

Von Tilzer, Albert, composer. "Take Me Out to the Ballgame." 1908.

Williams, William Carlos. "The Crowd at the Ball Game." *The Collected Poems of William Carlos Williams, Volume I, 1909–1939*. Ed. Christopher MacGowan. New York: New Directions, 1938.

Work History News Winter 2003.

Racial Attitudes towards Jews in the "Negro Leagues": The Case of Effa Manley

by Rebecca Alpert

By the time the United States entered World War II in 1941, Negro League baseball had developed into a profitable, respected, and mostly black-owned business. While many factors contributed to this development, some portion of the financial success was attributable to the contributions of Jewish entrepreneurs during the depression (Alpert; Lanctot). Notably, Ed Gottlieb, Abe Saperstein, and Syd Pollock were welcomed into the business because of the financial experience and expertise they were able to bring to bear. Still, these entrepreneuers were also frequently viewed warily by their black partners and competitors as both white and Jewish outsiders. Which brings us to a consideration of yet another owner, Effa Manley (1897–1981), who was also an obvious outsider—but in a different way—and what a difference this proved to be. This difference, in fact, has led to her being the only woman in history to be inducted into the Baseball Hall of Fame, which occurred in 2006, and the acknowledgment of the the unique role she played in the business of black baseball. From 1935-48, along with her husband Abe, she owned and operated the Newark Eagles, one of the most successful teams in the Negro National League.[1] Her husband started the team in Brooklyn, but moved it to Newark after an initial lackluster season in New York. By the end of that first season, Effa had taken over all of the front office business operations and was on her way to becoming an outspoken proponent and leader of Negro League baseball. Yet, although she lived her life as a black woman, her biological heritage was white. The intent of this article is to explore

19

the complicated relationship between Manley and those Jewish entrepreneurs who were both her allies and competitors in the business of the Negro Leagues and what, in turn, this complex relationship reveals about a dynamic period in the development of American Jewish culture in relation to black culture in the 1930s and 1940s.

Effa Manley. Courtesy National Baseball Hall of Fame Library, Cooperstown, New York.

Upon first consideration, it would seem that Effa Manley did not like Jews very much, especially those who were her competitors in baseball. In a July 28, 1941 letter to Seward Posey, business manager of the rival Homestead Grays, Manley suggested they make an alliance that could "stop Gottlieb, Wilkerson, Leuschner, Saperstein and all the other Jews who want to join them where Negro Baseball is concerned" (Letter to Posey).[2] She opined that if she or her husband were presiding over league business, "these Jews would be stopped in their tracks," noting that "the 10% Gottlieb puts in his pocket, and Saperstein puts in his, would set up a nice treasury" (ibid.). Manley was clearly playing off two common stereotypes about "these Jews"—their depiction as being both talented and greedy in the handling financial matters. In this case they are portrayed as having the inclination to make as much money as possible their first priority, rather than pursuing a full commitment to the advancement of this black business enterprise—and by extension the advancement of blacks in American society. Although in this instance Manley was thus invoking these stereotypes in a way that could be viewed as transparently and even virulently anti-Semitic, her actual relationships with Jews (in both her professional and personal life) reveal a more complex picture. Manley's attitudes towards Jews typify those prevalent in the black communities of the time—simultaneously negative and positive. While she deployed anti-Semitic rhetoric about Jews and money strategically, her comments also were, on occasion, indicative of her larger resentment of their financial power in the Negro Leagues. As a self-described "race woman," a common parlance of the time, she thought that the teams should be owned and operated by African-Americans. But she also understood that the Jews had a role to play in Negro baseball, and thus she was willing to welcome them as useful business partners and even as aspirational models for conducting business matters. And although Manley occasionally lumped them pejoratively together with other "ofays,"[3] her relationship with Jewish men in Negro baseball essentially reflected a paradoxical combination of wariness of, and enthusiasm for Jews, their financial acumen and economic status.

Manley's reaction to the Jewish entrepreneurs in the Negro Leagues should be understood in the context of her prior experiences with Jews—which also had both positive and negative aspects. It is likely that she had Jewish classmates when she was growing up in Philadelphia, attending the predominantly white William Penn High School for Girls (Rushing 21). She likely had additional personal experiences with Jews in Harlem, where she moved after finishing high school in 1916, and where Jews also lived and worked. She herself did not work in Harlem, but downtown in the millinery business, where it is also likely that she met similarly employed Jewish women in this gender-segregated industry.[4] Her first documented encounter with Jews, however, took place in the summer of 1934, when she took a leadership role in the "Don't Buy Where You Can't Work" campaign organized by the Citizens League for Fair Play against the Jewish owners of Blumstein's' Department Store on Harlem's 125th Street. This encounter taught her about working across the economic, social, and racial differences that existed between blacks and Jews. Through her work in this campaign, Manley learned the importance of blending political strategies in order to achieve success. She observed and participated in coalition work, public protest, behind-the-scenes negotiation, strategic use of rhetoric, press relations, and legislation. She would later use all of these political tools in order to make the Newark Eagles a successful business.[5]

Effa's background was working-class, and neither during her brief first marriage nor as a single working-woman was she welcomed in the upper echelons of Harlem's black society. But when she and her husband Abe married in 1933, Manley gained entrée into the black elite of Harlem, associating with the leaders of the community and the leading figures of the Harlem Renaissance. Abe had made his fortune in the illegal numbers business in Camden, New Jersey; and they had sufficient resources to live on "Sugar Hill" and socialize among wealthier and well-educated African Americans (Overmyer 12–16). In the winter of 1934, Manley organized the Harlem Women's Association.[6] One of its goals was to compel retail stores, owned primarily by Jewish merchants in Harlem's main shopping district on 125th Street, to hire African-American women in visible positions as sales clerks. According to Manley's recollections, William Davis, editor of the *Amsterdam News* gave her the idea to target Blumstein's. In recounting her experience some years later, she remembered Davis hinting that Mrs. Blumstein would be open to the suggestion that the store provide middle class jobs for better educated African-American women, given that they already employed blacks as elevator operators and in janitorial services (Marshall 86:13). When Mrs. Blumstein did not respond positively to the group's demands, Manley contacted the rector of St. Martin's Protestant Episcopal Church, John H. Johnson, to seek support (Letter to Banner). Johnson took over as the official leader of the organization, and gave it a new name: the "Citizens League for Fair Play." Manley was elected to the office of Secretary and was intimately involved in orchestrating the ensuing protest. The League's first tactic was to collect receipts from the store, mostly from St. Martin's parishioners, to demonstrate conclusively to the Blumstein's owners (both Mrs. L. M. Blumstein and her brother-in-law, William) that the vast majority of their sales came from African-American clientele. Johnson began the campaign on April 8, 1934 with a sermon asking his parishioners to bring their sales receipts to the church over a two-week period. Armed with the evidence that over seventy-five percent of the sales at Blumstein's came from black customers, Johnson met with William Blumstein. At the time, Johnson asked only that they train and hire one black woman as a sales clerk. Nonetheless, Blumstein refused (Johnson 68).

The League's response was to adopt a new and more aggressive public strategy. They held a mass meeting at the Church in May, at which they announced a boycott and picketing of the store under the banner "Don't Buy Where You Can't Work." The League gathered support, and evolved into a coalition of over three hundred civic, religious and business organizations, attracting a broad range of groups across the political spectrum. It included the integrationist-oriented Urban League as well as the NAACP. Those organizations, funded heavily by Jewish philanthropists, would normally pursue legal strategies rather than direct action; nonetheless, they lent their support to this campaign. Various groups of black nationalists also joined. One of their leaders, Sufi Abdul Hamid, had been involved in a similar effort that had been successful in changing retail-hiring practices in Chicago a year earlier. Hamid had already brought a militant version of those strategies to Harlem. Although these more radical leaders generally supported race-based, direct action strategies, their efforts were only grudgingly focused on employment opportunities for the middle class. Communist and Union groups were also involved, although they generally supported labor-oriented rather than racially-targeted strategies. That this coalition existed at all was remarkable, given the tensions that existed among these disparate groups. But any effort to increase black employment during the economic hardships created by the Depression was a high community priority (McKay 185, 191–92).

Harlem's two black newspapers were divided in their response. The League received strong backing from Fred Moore, the editor of the *New York Age*. *The Age* carried weekly articles about the League and the progress of the boycott, and this publicity was instrumental to their success. But William Davis, editor of the *Amsterdam News*, disapproved of their strategies and did not support or publicize the group's efforts. *News* columnists like George Schuyler worried that the picketing would backfire, alienate white businesses, and cause a loss of advertising revenue for the paper (Moreno 37).

The picketing and boycott lasted six weeks through mid-July, and was ultimately successful in persuading the Blumstein-ownership to meet with the League's leadership to seek a resolution. Johnson took Manley to the private meeting along with a lawyer, Richard Cary, and Fred Moore of the *Age*. Manley later recalled making an argument that she believed swayed Blumstein. She told him that he should show respect for black women, who deserved to work in the same jobs available to white women. Under current circumstances, she suggested, black women could only find work as maids or prostitutes. While her reference to prostitution might have been shocking, Blumstein might also have been disturbed by the reminder that most black domestics in Harlem labored in Jewish homes for poor wages. A few days later Blumstein agreed to hire several new clerks immediately, and promised that there would be twenty more at the beginning of the fall season. Although Blumstein's reneged on employing more black women in the fall, the store hired fifteen new sales clerks immediately, and the Citizens' League called off the boycott. Manley viewed the campaign against Blumstein's as a triumph. In her estimation, it had a critical impact on retail stores and employment for African-Americans on 125th Street, as other merchants, fearing similar actions against their stores, also hired a number of black staff (Marshall 86). Scholars suggest this effort succeeded not only as a short-term victory but also as the beginning of the mobilization of political and economic powers in Harlem (Greenberg 136).

Manley must also have been aware of later events that split the coalition and exposed tensions both intra-racial and between the Jewish merchants and more radical black leaders. When the *New York Age* published photographs of the new clerks, and they were seen to be all light-skinned, middle-class women, some of the coalition members became outraged. While Effa and her cohort did spend time on the picket lines (*New York Amsterdam News* July 7, 1934) it was all too clear that the working-class and darker skinned women, who were actually doing most of the picketing, would receive no direct or immediate benefit for their efforts. Some of the leaders, including Sufi Hamid and the Harlem Labor Union, decided to continue and broaden their picketing and boycotting efforts, despite the withdrawal of the other coalition members from doing so.

Although many of the Jewish merchants on 125th Street had heeded the message of the boycott and began to hire African-American workers, others who did not do so became the most visible targets of the continued picketing. Some of the invective against them was tinged with anti-Semitic rhetoric, including positive comparisons to Nazi boycotts of Jewish stores that had begun the previous year in Germany. The anti-Semitic angle was emphasized in the Jewish and New York daily press and Harlem's Jewish merchants appealed to Mayor Fiorello LaGuardia to stop the "anti-Semitic street corner agitation carried on by the black Hitler." Sufi Hamid was also condemned by the *Age* and *Amsterdam News* as a "Black Nazi" (Hunter 188; McKay 196, 198–204).[7]

The picketing and boycotting efforts exposed black-Jewish tensions in Harlem. In November 1934, after one of the merchants filed a lawsuit, a liberal Jewish judge reluctantly enjoined the picketing, ruling that it was only allowable as a legal tactic in cases of labor conflict but not in matters of race. These tensions continued, however, as black women still were relegated to working for low wages as domestics in Jewish homes, while Jewish merchants remained dominant in the retail business on 125th Street. Still, Jews at this time also took positive steps in support of the advancement of blacks. Many Jewish Harlem merchants, including the Blumsteins, were primary contributors to integrationist organizations such as the NAACP and the Urban League. The complicated relationships between blacks and Jews in Harlem provided the backdrop for how Manley came to understand the complex connections and differences between Jews and blacks in the Negro Leagues, in particular, and on the streets of Harlem, in general.

When writing to the Research Director of the Urban League about events surrounding the campaign in 1940, Manley provided her analysis of the cause of the problems:

> It is most unfortunate that Negroes must be thought of as Black people and so many other races as white people. If we could be thought of [as] The Negro Race, the same as French, Italian, Jewish and all the others, we might not suffer so. The Race has always proven extremely courageous and helpful in doing its part to maintain this glorious Country of ours, and yet are so unjustly discriminated against, because of the pigmentation of their skin alon[e]. (Letter to Banner)

The tenor of this language suggests an espousal of an integrationist strategy (through which blacks should be treated like other races), while simultaneously upholding a racially oriented pride that makes a point of marking out differences. Blacks, like Jews, Manley argued, should be allowed the opportunity to be both distinct and equal. This combination of separatist strategies, invoking racial pride, and the integrationist desire to be treated like other groups would characterize her relationship to her Jewish counterparts in black baseball. The lessons she learned from the boycott about how to negotiate with Jewish businessmen—and in the tactical use of anti-Semitic rhetoric—would serve as important business strategies for her.

Manley's use of pronouns in the quotation above adds another subtle dimension to understanding her successes in the world of business. Referring to blacks, she says both that "*we* might not suffer so" and yet refers to "the pigmentation of *their* skin." It is not until much later in her life that Manley revealed publicly that she knew herself to be biologically white. When researchers began to pay attention to the history of the Negro Leagues in the 1970s, Manley was most willing to discuss her experiences. She wrote a book about her life as a team owner and did several oral histories and many interviews with the press. Manley first revealed her racial heritage in several interviews in 1977 (Marshall 91; Kisner 47). She described herself as the illegitimate child of a German/Native-American mother (Bertha Ford) and a white father (John [either Isaac or Marcus] Bishop), attributing her parentage to an affair her mother had with her boss while married to John Brooks, which resulted in a lawsuit for alienated affections and subsequent divorce. Effa grew up assuming Brooks was her biological father. She was raised by her mother and her stepfather Benjamin Cole in a blended family consisting of Brooks' and Coles' six children. Everyone else in the family was black, and Effa identified with them growing up. Bertha did not revealed Effa's white parentage to her until she was a teenager.[8]

Living in a black family and neighborhoods growing up, identified as "colored" by census takers, and self-identifying as black throughout her life, Effa, it would be fair to say, was socially black and deeply connected to the African-American community, a self-conscious "race woman." She listed herself as "colored" on her marriage licenses and her (four) marriages—one early marriage that ended in a quick divorce, and two brief ones after Abe's death in 1952— were all to black men. Her extended family assumed she was of African descent, as did all of her social acquaintances in Harlem and her business associates in the Negro Leagues. She lived her life primarily in the black community, where she was accepted as black. But much after the manner of other light-skinned African-American women, she passed (or, as she put it, "traveled") as white when it served her interest. As already noted, she attended an inter-racial high school and made white friends at a time when the races rarely mixed. After moving to New York, she obtained jobs usually reserved for white (mostly Jewish immigrant) women in the millinery trade. She proudly related a story about Abe Manley buying her an engagement ring at Tiffany's where the sales clerk assumed she was white. When she traveled around the country she found it advantageous to pass as white in hotels and restaurants off-limits to her husband, who sometimes posed as her chauffeur. She also used her light-skinned privilege to purchase the home where she and Abe lived in Newark (Marshall 91). Living on both sides of the color-line gave Effa Manley a unique perspective and understanding of racial categories, and probably factored into her view that blacks were a race no different from Jews, while simultaneously increasing her awareness of the cultural differences in each community.[9]

The strategies that Effa Manley learned in the challenge to Blumstein's, as well as her complex, racial self-identity, helped define her relationships within the National Negro League. In particular, her heightened awareness of race would be a contributing factor in her relationships with the Jewish owners and booking agents she met in 1935, when Abe purchased the Brooklyn Eagles, and developed further, when she subsequently took over the business side of the team. Manley was concerned that the black owners of the teams in the

Negro League did not handle business matters as well as she would have liked. Awareness of the successes of Jewish businesses in Harlem affected the way she interpreted racial differences. As she wrote in confidence to Wendell Smith, the sports writer for the *Pittsburgh Courier*:

> [W]e Negroes are not trained in business administration (some races do not seem to need any training).... We realize we do not know ourselves, and we let people lead us who have other thoughts in mind. Mainly making money.... (Letter to Smith)

Surely she was thinking about the Jewish philanthropists and businessmen in Harlem when referencing "the races [that] do not seem to need any training" and who are mostly interested in "making money." Manley was both impressed by their talents and lamented that blacks had neither the same "innate" capacity nor access to learning business skills. This dual view was manifest most clearly in her dealings with Ed Gottlieb. In certain respects Ed and Effa were in similar positions. In the business of the Negro National League both were outsiders: Effa was the only woman, Gottlieb was the only Jew, and neither was completely white or black in terms of the social milieu of the time. Both were silent partners: co-owners who handled the business side of their respective teams, the Philadelphia Stars and the Newark Eagles. While black-owner Ed Bolden (for the Stars) and Effa's husband Abe (for the Eagles) were the public faces of their respective teams, Gottlieb and Effa were both also officers (or, in Effa's case, her husband's surrogate) in the Negro National League and did a good deal of business together. Effa and Ed generally got along well. They conducted routine financial transactions cordially, even if, as we will soon see, they sometimes found themselves on opposite sides in arguments over policies and plans.

In the correspondence in the Newark Eagles Collection, everyone addressed Effa deferentially as Mrs. Manley. While she often wrote to other owners on a first-name basis, as they did to one another, letters to Ed (known to his friends as "Gotty") always began "Dear Gottlieb." Their conversations in this idiom were primarily business-like and polite, but also provide glimpses of a closer working relationship. Most of the letters dealt with mundane matters: problems with umpires, deliberations over the value of rain-insurance, improving publicity and providing passes for Effa's parents when the Eagles played in Philadelphia. She also contacted him for advice about other business: asking his opinion about starting her own basketball team, working together on a plan to handle the problems of gas-rationing during the War, and serving as a committee of two to draft the league's constitution (Letter to Gottlieb, October 21, 1942; Negro League Minutes). Sometimes she complained to him about the other owners. She was quoted in the *Afro-American* as admiring Gottlieb's business abilities; a fact she confirmed several times in the course of their correspondence, as when she wrote, "I know you can do more to get things straight than any one else in this Organization" (*Baltimore Afro-American*; Letter to Gottlieb, May 14, 1941). But she also let Gottlieb know that she did not think he really had the best interests of Negro baseball at heart, and wished he would use his business talents to advance the league. As she wrote after the 1942 season:

> Let's don't quarrel. I still think what I did a few years ago. You have all the ability necessary to put Negro Baseball on a permanent paying basis. But in order to do this Negro Baseball must come first, and Ed Gottlieb second. Is this too much to hope for? (Letter to Gottlieb, November 7, 1942)

Her words here could be interpreted as reflecting a simplistic stereotype of Jews, as being both good with finances yet really only interested in making money for themselves, thus placing Gottlieb as the outsider and herself as an insider committed to black baseball. Although she worked closely with Gottlieb and sought his advice, she also frequently questioned the strength of his commitment to black baseball, about which she claimed to care deeply, while protesting that he did not. But the major quarrel between Gottlieb and Manley revealed that what she defined as Gottlieb's self-interest may, in fact, have benefited the league more than she was willing to admit. While Manley accepted Gottlieb in his role as owner and Negro National League officer, their one significant quarrel was over Gottlieb's position as the League's booking agent for Yankee Stadium. She objected to his power to decide how to use this important venue that generated a good deal of income for league teams—but especially additional revenue for Gottlieb.

Mostly, Manley objected to Gottlieb's promotion strategy to showcase the premier Negro League pitcher, Satchel Paige. Gottlieb put together a deal with Yankees general manager Ed Barrow for five Negro League doubleheaders at Yankee Stadium in 1939. Gottlieb's arrangement saved the league $12,500 in rental fees. For his work, Gottlieb received a ten percent booking fee. The owners had all agreed to Gottlieb taking the percentage when he took on the Yankee Stadium promotion. Although the Manleys initially opposed giving Gottlieb the commission, they ultimately participated in the lucrative arrangement. Gottlieb, as promoter, put up all the advance money, and the clubs involved gained an aggregate total of over $16,000 in profits for themselves. For his work, Gottlieb received a total of $1,100 (*Chicago Defender* July 16, 1938; *Pittsburgh Courier* February 4, 1939; Rust 54).

In 1940, the New York owners—James Semler of the New York Black Yankees and Alex Pompez of the New York Cubans—joined the Manleys in their objection to Gottlieb's exclusive control of Yankee Stadium promotions. At the winter meetings of the Negro National League they banded together to fight the reelection of Tom Wilson (owner of the Baltimore Elite Giants and Gottlieb's close associate) as Negro National League President, because in their opinion, he was too weak to stand up to Gottlieb. Semler, Pompez, and Abe Manley saw Gottlieb's booking of Yankee Stadium as an incursion into their territory, for which they at least should have been compensated and/or brought in as partners. Semler, Pompez and Manley further argued that they, not Gottlieb, should get the ten percent booking fee. Supported by Wilson and Cumberland "Cum" Posey of the Homestead Grays, Gottlieb fought back, arguing that the New York owners "were in the same position as a patient who applies for medical aid and then curses out the doctor when he charges him a sum for curing him" (*New York Amsterdam News* February 24, 1940; *Pittsburgh Courier* February 10, 1940).

Effa Manley escalated the debate with remarks she made at a League meeting that were later reported in the black press. She was quoted as saying that this was "something bigger than a little money! We are fighting for a Race issue. In other words what we are doing here has become more important than we [are]." Manley's comments were dismissed by some due to her gender, and Posey was reported to have left the room in anger, refusing to return until Abe Manley promised to leave his wife home "where she belonged" (*Chicago Defender* February 10, 1940).

Gottlieb also received support on this matter from the black press. Fay Young did not approve of Effa Manley bringing up race at a time when whites were beginning to pay attention to black baseball (*Chicago Defender* February 10, 1940). Art Carter defended Gottlieb as a businessman who was entitled to do the best he could for himself and not obligated to be more financially equitable to serve the common good. Ultimately, the problem was settled through compromise. Gottlieb was reprimanded and removed as recording secretary but allowed to keep the Yankee Stadium promotions. With Gottlieb doing the booking, the Manleys chose not to play in Yankee Stadium in 1940 in protest. Yet Effa Manley thought it wise to retract her statements about the racial nature of the disagreement. When asked whether she opposed white ownership, she replied, "Certainly not. Some white owners are the best of men. I even admire Gottlieb's business ability. He would be all right if the chairman [Tom Wilson] could handle him. He needs to be whipped into line" (*Baltimore Afro-American*). Manley was sincere about her antipathy to Wilson, whom she frequently tried to remove as the President of the League. She eventually persuaded the League to retain her former colleague in the Citizens League, the Reverend John Johnson, as League president in 1947. He thus became the first independent non-owner to hold that position. Johnson had chaired the committee on integrating baseball established by Mayor LaGuardia in 1945, and as League President worked to make Major League baseball acknowledge responsibility for its part in destroying the Negro Leagues, which was an unintended consequence of integration, as African-American fans changed their allegiance from the Negro Leagues to teams like the Brooklyn Dodgers, Cleveland Indians, and New York Giants who were showcasing black star players (Lanctot 307–08).

When she was interviewed in the 1970s, Effa claimed that it was her husband who was interested in helping the New York owners get the Yankee Stadium rental contract. She stated that she was more willing to work with men like Gottlieb, calling them "fair and decent," although she was also quite critical of booking-agents in her autobiography (Holway 321; Manley and Hardwick 50). Evidence suggests that Effa was sincere. Despite the strategic rhetoric about his self-interest and the anti-Semitic nuance to her remarks, Effa's problems with Ed Gottlieb were not primarily about his being Jewish or his lack of commitment to the league, or about the New York teams' rights to their territory. She used racially-tinged rhetoric strategically to support her husband's allegiances, knowing that his allies from Harlem would resonate with that kind of coded language. But the true reason for her personal anger toward Gottlieb's Yankee Stadium promotions was probably more about what she thought to be the disrespectful attitude aimed at her by Satchel Paige, who was by far the most famous Negro baseball star. Showcasing Paige in order to attract crowds was something Manley could not easily stomach. Manley was still angry that, although the Eagles purchased Paige's contract in 1938 for what in those times was the high price of $5000, Paige refused to report to Newark, preferring instead to jump to Latin American leagues. When he finally returned to the United States, he still did not honor his obligation to report to Newark, but instead began to pitch for his own barnstorming "Satchel Paige All-Stars" and subsequently for J. L. Wilkinson's Kansas City Monarchs. Paige, due to his celebrity, saw no reason why he should be forced to play by the rules—especially the rules as dictated by owners. Moreover, the other owners refused to support Manley, and this too gave her good reason for not taking part in using Paige to promote the League. Indeed, she was also angry because Paige was at the time actually playing in the Negro American League, so his services would consequently have to be "rented" for the New York dates. Manley deemed that an unacceptable and undignified practice that undermined the integrity of the league.

Gottlieb showed no interest in tolerating what he considered to be Manley's petty, personal grudge. He believed, pragmatically, that showcasing Satchel Paige was the key to promoting black baseball to white audiences. Gottlieb arranged with Black Yankee's owner Jim Semler to pay Paige $300 to pitch. He explained to Manley that this "was very cheap, as he was largely responsible for the crowd, and helped all of us to make money." He wrote several letters trying to convince her of how important this was to the League and to the other owners, arguing that Paige's presence would "help Semler get a crowd, and get out of debt." He further argued that this promotion could not "possibly hurt you or anyone else." Gottlieb reasoned that Paige, pitching in an exhibition game, would not disrupt the Eagles' fan base in Newark, but it *would* make new fans for the Negro National League (Letter to Manley, May 16, 1941; Letter to Manley, July 21, 1941). She replied "If [the] Yankees use Satchell please arrange for the Eagles . . . to play in Baltimore. I certainly could not be asked to play with Satchell pitching against us after all the devil I went through about him . . . he cost me a lot of cash and embarrassment" (Letter to Gottlieb, May 14, 1941).

When all was said and done, Gottlieb's position was vindicated. The exhibition went on, Paige was paid $300, each club made $844, and the white press took note of the Negro Leagues (Gottlieb, Letter to Manley, July 21, 1941). Nonetheless, Effa refused to pay her share of the expenses. The idea of paying Paige sent her into a rage against "the powers that are," who "certainly don't mind showing how little respect they have for us" (Letter to Posey, July 28, 1941). It was this incident that triggered her angry letter, noted above, to Seward Posey suggesting that they make an alliance that could "stop Gottlieb, Wilkerson, Leuschner, Saperstein and all the other Jews who want to join them where Negro Baseball is concerned" (Letter to Posey, July 28, 1941). Manley's use of racial rhetoric was a result of her anger at what she considered disrespect to the integrity of a black business. Reacting as a race woman, she used a racial argument to emphasize her strong opposition.

Gottlieb, however, believed he was doing the right thing and continued to insist that Manley behave responsibly: ". . . as to our personal account, I really hoped that you would agree to pay your share of the Satchell Paige money, as I am sure I doubled each club's share by making the change, and figured a personal conversation with you would do the trick" (Letter to Manley, October 11, 1941). But Manley held her ground: "How can I pay Satchell when I paid Wilkerson for him and never got it back? . . . To ask me to pay for Satchell's services is just too much. . . . I should get paid for letting someone else use him" (Letter to Gottlieb, November 4, 1941). The following year the account still remained unsettled. Gottlieb owed the league money from Satchel Paige's appearances in Yankee Stadium but would not release the funds until the Manleys paid their share. But Effa did not relent:

> . . . when a person in this baseball [league] paid some hard cash for a ballplayer and just had him taken from him by plain strength, and the offending party makes as much money with him as Wilkie did with Satchell, he should at least give us back the cash we paid for him. (Letter to Gottlieb, December 15, 1941)

From Gottlieb's perspective, it was her recalcitrance and not his management style that was holding back the financial benefit for the league. He reminded her that she admitted they made much more money with Paige there, even after paying his fee, than they would have without him. Although she continued to refuse to pay for his appearances, the following year she softened her opposition and even requested that he pitch when the Eagles played against the Monarchs (Gottlieb, Letter to Manley, November 10, 1942; Manley, Letter to Baird, June 8, 1943).

After this encounter, however, Manley's relationship with Gottlieb took on a more competitive tone. She began to book her own games in New York's Polo Grounds, even when they were in direct competition with the games Gottlieb had booked for League teams in nearby Yankee Stadium (Manley, Letter to Posey, August 25, 1941). She continued to try to have the Yankee Stadium booking contract taken away from Gottlieb. She worked with others involved in the League, led by *Norfolk Journal and Guide* sports editor Lem Graves, who also expressed a desire to get "the Jews" out of power (Manley, Letter to Graves).

But even though Manley claimed to object to the presence of "Jews" in the league to colleagues to whom she believed that strategy had an appeal, she continued to work behind the scenes with Jewish promoters to advance the interests of the Newark Eagles. In the winter of 1942 she began a relationship with Abe Saperstein and Syd Pollock, who were owners and booking agents for the Negro American League that was based in the Midwest. During the off-season, annoyed with Gottlieb and the other Negro National League owners, who supported him, Effa contemplated leaving the league and having the Newark Eagles play independent baseball instead. She contacted Saperstein about becoming their agent and promoter. The Manleys even announced to the black press that they were considering withdrawing from the league. They did not reveal that they had consulted with Saperstein but suggested their dissatisfaction with Gottlieb was the main reason that they might decide to become independent. Saperstein responded enthusiastically, asking if she would be willing to fly out to see him in Chicago. By the time Manley replied by mail two days later, they had already spoken by phone. In her letter she acknowledged that the move outside league play would give the other owners the ability to sign Eagle players with impunity, but she was willing to take that risk "to tie up with someone [like Saperstein] who knows the ropes" (Saperstein, Telegram to Manley; Manley, Letter to Saperstein, February 22, 1942).

Sensing the urgency of the deal, Saperstein suggested that Pollock, his associate, make the trip from his home in North Tarrytown, New York to talk to Effa and her husband. Pollock was not only Saperstein's associate, but the proprietor of the comedy baseball team, the Ethiopian Clowns. Like the other owners, Manley expressed distress over the antics and politics of Pollock's team. In a 1944 letter to Negro American League owner B. B. Martin she wrote in reference to Pollock, "those people never did want baseball to get too high class, and all these sorts of things help to keep it down." But later in life she admitted: "I didn't like the Ethiopian Clowns. I wanted baseball to be dignified. One day when they were playing in New York I decided to go see them, and nobody laughed louder than I did. So after that I stopped complaining" (Holway 321).

Despite her reservations about the Clowns, Effa welcomed Pollock into the Manley's home in Newark. In his lengthy letter of introduction that confirmed the visit, he told them he planned to supply them with facts and figures that would convince them to work through Saperstein's office and "eliminate many headaches, squabbles at league meetings, and make yourself just as much money . . . if not more than you ever did playing league ball." Pollock went on to say that "Saperstein and his staff in the Chicago office outshine all others" at booking and promoting. He emphasized that the Eagles "would fit perfectly into plans Saperstein has in mind and briefly outlined to me several weeks ago when he was in NYC" (Saperstein, Letter to Manley, February 24, 1942; Pollock, Letter to Manley, February 26, 1942).

Saperstein made a strong argument that plans for joining a new league would serve the Newark Eagles well. In Pollock's summary of their conversation he reinforced Effa's desire to "lick Posey and his motives" and divest "Cum Posey of the power he has edged himself into." Although Effa blamed Gottlieb for her desire to leave the League, when discussing the matter in public, she was also aware that Seward and Posey were most often Gottlieb's allies in the Negro National League, not hers. Pollock added fuel to the fire, suggesting that Manley permit the Clowns to use Ruppert Park when the Eagles were traveling. They would both make a "nice bit of change" and "it would be a blow at Posey and a knockout punch I think you'd like to deliver." Clearly Manley was willing to work with anyone she believed would help her make the Eagles a successful enterprise, regardless of ethnic identity (Pollock, Letter to Manley, February 28, 1942).

As it turned out, nothing came of Pollock's visit or invitation, and the Newark Eagles stayed in the Negro National League. Two weeks later, Saperstein sent Manley a note wishing her the best of luck. He left the door open for further conversation, saying he "would welcome word from time to time as to how you progress," and suggested that they get together when he was in New York, touring with his comedy basketball team, the Harlem Globetrotters. A few days later, he received a cordial reply that made it clear her husband wanted to stay with the league (Saperstein, Letter to Manley, March 7, 1942; Manley, Letter to Saperstein, March 11, 1942; Saperstein, Letter to Manley, March 14, 1942).

Manley continued to work with Saperstein to book games for the Eagles in the Midwest, turning down a similar offer from Posey to do the booking. In 1944 Saperstein booked the Eagles to play at Wrigley Field, another major league stadium where Saperstein made the rental agreements. The following year Effa again made arrangements with Saperstein, this time for the Birmingham Black Barons and Kansas City Monarchs to come to Newark. Although she still disliked having to pay extra for having Paige pitch, she did accept the offer when Kansas City played Newark in 1945, calling her previous concerns for compensation "water under the bridge as everyone is trying to do the best he can today." Ultimately, Manley proved to be a pragmatic business owner who showed she could come to understand the importance of compromise for the sake of financial benefit (Letter to Baird, June 27, 1945).

Manley also avoided dealing with Gottlieb, directly, booking with agents like Brady Johnson in Virginia, and A. J. Hammonds in North Carolina.

Hammonds, in particular, indicated to her that he also preferred "working with my own people in this promotion, rather than working with the Jewish people" (Hammonds). But Manley herself continued to work with "the Jewish people," booking games against the Clowns to play in Florida before the opening of the season and continuing, despite her reservations, to work with Gottlieb to book games with his own team, the Philadelphia Stars (Manley, Letter to Pollock).

It should thus be clear that Effa Manley was quite willing to work with Jews if this meant the possibility of advancing the interests of her own team. Yet, by the same token, it is also clear that she showed no hesitation to resort to anti-Semitic rhetoric in certain circumstances, if she thought this served her interests. But in the final analysis she also understood the importance of the Jewish promoters and was perfectly content to work with them.

Her willingness to engage with Jews to advance her business interests and her comfort around them is underlined further by her relationship with a law student at Newark University, Jerome Kessler, whom she employed to do publicity. As she later described it, "There was a young Jewish lawyer, Jerome Kessler, who had helped finance his law school training handling publicity for the Eagles." Kessler continued in the Manley's employ after passing the bar in 1940. On Kessler's stationery he listed himself as "Press Relations Director" of the Newark Eagles (Kessler, January 1, 1940). His correspondence with Effa indicated a strong personal connection and a marked enthusiasm for the opportunity to write and place stories about the team in the press. Kessler helped Manley gain what she wanted, attention from the white press in Newark, which she assumed would be more responsive to a white publicity agent. For her part, Manley withstood criticism from the black press for hiring a Jew in this role, given that there were so few white-collar jobs available to blacks at the time. To some of the other owners, it seemed hypocritical on her part to hire Kessler while criticizing other Negro League teams for working with men like Gottlieb (*New Jersey Herald News* Sports Editor Brown; Carter). But as someone who passed for white on more than one occasion, she knew the advantages of having a white person responsible for getting the word out about her team to the white "dailies." Jerry Kessler embraced this role with enthusiasm.

Effa and Jerry kept up their close relationship over a considerable period of time. When applying for the Naval Reserve, for example, he requested a detailed letter from her as the "person to whom I am directly responsible in my current employment," attesting to his good character. She addressed her letters to him, "Dear Jerry," and in them they discussed their visits both at home and in the office. After passing the bar, and while serving in the armed services, he began to do legal work for the Eagles, communicating with the head of the Mexican Baseball League, Jorge Pasqual, gathering information about Workmen's Compensation in Pennsylvania and New Jersey, and negotiating other insurance matters. Kessler accompanied Manley to court when she was sued by former Eagles player Daltrie Cooper after he broke his ankle during a game and was dropped from the team. She and Kessler discussed player-contracts. She sought his solace over a letter she got from "that nut Satchell Paige." He helped with plans for bringing the mayor of Newark to the park for opening day, and worked with her on scheduling games (Manley, Letter to Kessler, May 15, 1940; *Pittsburgh Courier* August 17, 1940; Manley, Letter to Kessler, January 23, 1941; March 3, 1941; March 4, 1941; March 15, 1941; April 15, 1941; June 2, 1941).

Most of their correspondence was, of course, about publicity, and Kessler communicated with all of the black newspapers as well as with the local white press. There is a hiatus in the correspondence during part of Kessler's army service in the Signal Corps. But when he got back in touch on his return, her reply described how much she missed his work and how inadequate his replacement as publicity man had turned out to be. She asked him if he thought the Army would mind if he sent out some publicity to the [white] "dailies" while still in the service (Kessler, Letter to Manley; Manley, Letter to Kessler, February 25, 1944).

After the War, when Kessler was a practicing attorney in Newark, Manley went to him for help solving another problem. Effa was one of the only two Negro League owners (Ed Gottlieb being the other) to publicly criticize Branch Rickey's refusal to pay the Negro League owners for the players he signed up for the Dodgers, and she enlisted Kessler to help her make her case (Letter to Gottlieb, June 25, 1946; Holway 325). Rickey made it known that he felt no need to deal with the Negro League owners and had nothing but contempt for them and their style of business. He claimed that, since their players were not under contract to the teams, he had the right to negotiate directly with the players and to by-pass the Negro League owners. When Rickey began to make overtures to the Eagles' Monte Irvin, who was under contract to the Eagles, Effa turned to Kessler: "I called him and told him Mr. Rickey had no business taking all these people. I asked him if he would gamble with me on making an issue of it." Rickey dropped his pursuit of Irvin because of Kessler's legal efforts. Feeling that she had wronged Irvin by taking away his opportunity to play for the Dodgers, she asked Kessler to contact other teams to see if they would be interested in purchasing Irvin's contract. He contacted the Yankees and then the New York Giants, who subsequently signed Irvin and paid the Eagles $5000 for his contract. Manley willingly paid Kessler fifty percent of the profit that she agreed was due him for his labors (Manley and Hardwick 90–92).

In conclusion, Effa Manley's attitude about Jewish involvement in the league must be contextualized and should be seen as part of a business strategy she used to protect her interests and to facilitate her alliances. Based on what she learned in the "Don't Buy Where You Can't Work" campaign, she recognized the value of using anti-Semitic rhetoric with those she suspected harbored separationist tendencies, whenever she thought this might be strategically useful. Although she lived as a black woman in the Negro Leagues, she also relied on her white identity to overcome the barriers of gender. To no small extent, she probably identified with the ambivalent position of the Jewish men she worked with everyday, seeing herself as their equal, since like her, they were part insiders and part outsiders. Her working relationships with Gottlieb, Saperstein, Pollock, and Kessler illustrate that Effa Manley believed the stereotypes of her day: That Jews had an inherent talent for dealing with money and handling business, while, in contrast, blacks did not naturally possess this talent. She respected the business acumen of Jews, and their ability to cross racial lines to help the league and she was more than willing to work with them. She may have harbored stereotypes about Jews and money but they did not keep her from having respectful working relationships with them, and may have been part of her motivation for doing so.

It was clear to Effa and the other owners that the Negro Leagues could not survive the integration of Major League baseball. The Manleys sold the Newark Eagles in 1948. Abe died in 1952. Effa spent her remaining years living with her family of origin in Philadelphia and later in Los Angeles. When the Negro Leagues became a subject of interest to baseball researchers, Effa devoted time and energy to sharing her legacy, publishing an autobiography, participating in several oral history projects, and lobbying the Baseball Hall of Fame to recognize the contributions of Negro League players—an effort that eventually bore fruit. While she continued to associate with Negro League players, in her later life she had no contact with the Jewish men with whom she worked (Overmyer 247–59).

The ways in which Effa Manley so freely indulged in stereotypical language is something that we can easily criticize today as being both jarring and offensive. But such twenty-first century judgments of Effa Manley are anachronistic and thus to some extent far too simplistic. It is far wiser to examine her life in baseball, as we have endeavored to do above, from a more nuanced perspective. She shared a good deal with her Jewish business colleagues, especially in terms of the ambiguity of her social position in the 1930s and 1940s. She is revealed to be a woman who was not quite black who competed with men who, from the standpoint of the day, were not quite lily-white. These were men she both disparaged and admired. Above all else, she viewed all the men in her life in baseball—black, white and Jewish—as her equals, and she took every opportunity to make sure that they knew this as well.

Notes

1. Two book-length works tell the story of the Newark Eagles. See the excellent studies by Luke and Overmyer.
2. Unless otherwise indicated, correspondence in this article is taken from the Newark Eagles Papers.
3. A derogatory, slang term for a white person whose etymological origin is unclear. See, e.g., "Ofay."
4. Greenberg points out an advertisement for an African-American clothing store with headline "American Negroes Competing against Jews in Haberdashery World" ("Or Does It Explode" 117). She further suggests that black women before the Depression were "independent and self-reliant" and often were hired for "gender segregated work [including seamstresses] ... better educated worked ... sometimes as shop clerks, or in rare cases, businesswomen" (Greenberg, *To Ask for an Equal Chance* 9).
5. For a basic outline of the events involved in the Harlem "Don't Buy Where You Can't Work" campaign and their aftermath, see Greenberg; Hunter; Johnson; McKay; and Moreno. The following overall discussion of the campaign is based on these sources.
6. According to Hunter (183), Sufi Abdul Hamdi launched a street offensive and "Effa Manley of the Harlem Housewives Association, shocked at the ferocity of Sufi's movement, sent a call to Harlem's ministers to organize a 'respectable' job campaign. Reverend John H. Johnson, a former Columbia basketball star and vicar of St. Martin's Episcopal Church, was the first to reply."
7. McKay claims charges of anti-Semitism were trumped up to set these two minorities against each other, "Negroes certainly draw no line between the Jews and other whites" (208). Like Manley, he looked at Jewish labor organizing as an aspirational model (217–18).
8. Rushing found Manley's birth registration to be: "Ethel Ford, March 27, 1897, female, black, 1840 Carlisle St., 26 Ward, Parents: John and Bertha Ford," Occ Clerk, The Philadelphia City Archives, Philadelphia, PA. He noted that there was no "John Ford"—the name was inserted to cover her illegitimacy. Rushing also argues that Brooks was a criminal, and he could find no documentation that Brooks ever sued Bishop, a central piece of the story Manley told in the 1970s about her birth.
9. As Kaplan points out, while whites saw this kind of passing as a moral dilemma, for blacks it was an ethical triumph (273). See also Alexander 83–94.

Works Cited

Alexander, Lisa Doris. "Effa Manley and the Politics of Passing." *Black Ball: A Journal of the Negro Leagues* 1.2 (Fall 2008): 83–94.

Alpert, Rebecca. *Out of Left Field: Jews and Black Baseball.* New York: Oxford Univ., 2011.

Baltimore Afro-American 27 April 1940.

Brown, Oliver "Butts." Letter to Effa Manley. 14 April 1940. Newark Eagle Papers. Newark Public Library, Newark, NJ [NEP].

Carter, Art. "From the Bench." *Baltimore Afro-American* 10 Feb. 1940.

Chicago Defender 16 July 1938.

Chicago Defender 10 Feb. 1940.

Gottlieb, Ed. Letter to Effa Manley. 16 May 1941. NEP.

———. Letter to Effa Manley. 21 July 1941. NEP.

———. Letter to Effa Manley. 11 Oct. 1941. NEP.

———. Letter to Effa Manley. 10 Nov. 1942. NEP.

Greenberg, Cheryl Lynn. *"Or Does It Explode?" Black Harlem in the Great Depression.* New York: Oxford Univ., 1991.

———. *To Ask for an Equal Chance: African Americans in the Great Depression.* Lanham, MD: Rowman & Littlefield, 2009.

Hammonds, A. J. Letter to Effa Manley. 24 Feb. 1945. NEP.

Holway, John. *Voices from the Great Black Baseball Leagues.* Rev. ed. New York: Da Capo, 1992.

Hunter, Gary Jerome. "Don't Buy from Where You Can't Work": Black Urban Boycott Movements During the Depression, 1929–41." Diss. Univ. of Michigan, 1977.

Johnson, John Howard. "Don't Buy Where You Can't Work." *Harlem: The War, and Other Addresses.* New York: Malliet, 1942. 60–68.

Kaplan, Carla. *Miss Anne in Harlem: The White Women of the Black Renaissance.* New York: HarperCollins, 2013.

Kessler, Jerome. Letter to Effa Manley. 23 Feb. 1944. NEP.

———. 1 Jan 1940. NEP.

Kisner, Ronald. "White Widow of Black Baseball Pioneer Writes Book about Saga." *Jet Magazine* 3 Mar. 1977: 46–48.

Lanctot, Neil. *Negro League Baseball: The Rise and Ruin of a Black Institution.* Philadelphia: Univ. of Pennsylvania, 2004.

Luke, Bob. *The Most Famous Woman in Baseball: Effa Manley and the Negro Leagues.* Washington, D.C.: Potomac, 2011.

Manley, Effa. Letter to Tom Baird. 8 June 1943. NEP.

———. Letter to Tom Baird. 27 June 1945. NEP.

———. Letter to Warren Banner. 8 May 1940. NEP.

———. Letter to Ed Gottlieb. 14 May 1941. NEP.

———. Letter to Ed Gottlieb. 4 Nov. 1941. NEP.

———. Letter to Ed Gottlieb. 15 Dec. 1941. NEP.
———. Letter to Ed Gottlieb. 7 Nov. 1942. NEP.
———. Letter to Ed Gottlieb. 25 June 1946. NEP.
———. Letter to Lem Graves. 25 Aug. 1941. NEP.
———. Letter to Jerome Kessler. 15 May 1940. NEP.
———. Letter to Jerome Kessler. 23 Jan. 1941. NEP.
———. Letter to Jerome Kessler. 3 Mar. 1941. NEP.
———. Letter to Jerome Kessler. 4 Mar. 1941. NEP.
———. Letter to Jerome Kessler. 15 Mar. 1941. NEP.
———. Letter to Jerome Kessler. 15 April 1941. NEP.
———. Letter to Jerome Kessler. 2 June 1941. NEP.
———. Letter to Jerome Kessler. 25 Feb. 1944. NEP.
———. Letter to Syd Pollock. 6 Feb. 1946. NEP.
———. Letter to Seward Posey. 28 July 1941. NEP.
———. Letter to Seward Posey. 25 Aug. 1941. NEP.
———. Letter to Abe Saperstein. 22 Feb. 1942. NEP.
———. Letter to Abe Saperstein. 11 Mar. 1942. NEP.
———. Letter to Wendell Smith. 7 Feb. 1944. NEP.
Manley, Effa, and Leon Herbert Hardwick. *Negro Baseball . . . before Integration.* Haworth, NJ: St. Johann, 1976.
Marshall, William. Interview with Effa Manley. Louie B. Nunn Center for Oral History, Univ. of Kentucky. 19 Oct. 1977.
McKay, Claude. *Harlem: Negro Metropolis.* New York: Dutton, 1940.
Moreno, Paul D. *From Direct Action to Affirmative Action: Fair Employment Law and Policy in America, 1933–1972.* Baton Rouge: Louisiana State Univ., 1997.
Negro League Minutes. 12 Mar. 1946. NEP.
New York Amsterdam News 7 July 1934.
New York Amsterdam News 24 Feb. 1940.
"Ofay." *Merriam-Webster.* N. d. 13 Aug 2014 <http://www.merriam-webster.com/dictionary/ofay>.
Overmyer, James. *Effa Manley and the Newark Eagles.* Metuchen, NJ: Scarecrow, 1993.
Pittsburgh Courier 4 Feb. 1939.
Pittsburgh Courier 10 Feb. 1940.
Pittsburgh Courier 17 Aug. 1940.
Pollock, Syd. Letter to Effa Manley. 26 Feb. 1942. NEP.
———. Letter to Effa Manley. 28 Feb. 1942. NEP.
Rushing, Lawrence H. " 'A Black Woman and Proud': Effa Manley and Racial Self-Identification." *Black Ball: A Journal of the Negro Leagues* 4.2 (Fall 2011): 17–35, 99.
Rust, Art. *"Get that Nigger off the Field!" A Sparkling, Informal History of the Black Man in Baseball.* New York: Delacorte, 1976.
Saperstein, Abe. Letter to Effa Manley. 24 Feb. 1942. NEP.

———. Letter to Effa Manley. 7 Mar. 1942. NEP.
———. Letter to Effa Manley. 14 Mar. 1942. NEP.
———. Telegram to Effa Manley. 20 Feb. 1942. NEP.

American Jewish Women on the Court: Seeking an Identity in Tennis in the Early Decades of the Twentieth Century*

by Linda J. Borish

INTRODUCTION

In the early decades of the twentieth century, as eastern European Jews immigrated to the United States, a stereotype of Jewish physical inferiority became prominent in American society. As noted in articles elsewhere in this volume, American Jews promoted sports for men as a way to challenge this stereotype, largely because most Americans associated athletic competition with masculine identity. Even though the stereotypical "Jewish" athlete was clearly male—as the Jewish press, institutions, and communities promoted male athleticism as a way for Jews to integrate into society as productive Americans—nonetheless, Jewish women also participated in the American sporting world during the inter-war period. Most notably, several Jewish women succeeded at the highest levels of competitive tennis and thus contributed to a reassessment of the national perspective on Jewish identity. The most famous of these women was Helen Jacobs, but there were also Clara Greenspan, Baroness Giacomo Levi, Millicent Hirsch, among others, who won victories on the court and praise off the court within both gender and Jewish contexts. The American press and the American Jewish press, in particular, shaped the popular perceptions of these American Jewish women tennis players. This, in turn, gave these talented American Jewish sportswomen the opportunity, as I have argued elsewhere, to challenge stereotypical views of American Jewish

---

* I thank Ari Sclar for his encouragement and suggestions on my article. I also appreciate the editors of the journal providing insightful comments.

women as lacking athletic ability, being physically weak, and generally disinterested in sporting activities (Borish, "'An Interest in Physical Well-Being'"; "'Athletic Activities of Various Kinds'"; "Jewish Sportswomen").

In an article in Pittsburgh's *Jewish Criterion* entitled "Lights of New York," on August 31, 1934, Martha Neumark stated, "The athletic fields of New York and immediate vicinity now have indelibly stamped upon them the marks of the prowess of a trio of Jewish women." Neumark further asserted, "Their phenomenal exploits are destroying for all time the pallid, sentimental picture of the Jewish woman perennially stagnant in the kitchen or nursery." In referring to Helen Hull Jacobs' victory at the United States Women's Singles Championship in New York, the journalist hailed her accomplishments (28). Jacobs and other American Jewish women-athletes paved the way for future Jewish tennis players such as Gladys Heldman and her daughter Julie Heldman, and helped facilitate tennis's opening up to other ethnic and minority groups (Borish, "Jewish American Women" 106). Using primary sources, especially American Jewish periodicals such as the *Jewish Criterion, The Sentinel, The American Hebrew*, and the mainstream American press such as the *New York Times, Los Angeles Times, Chicago Tribune*, among other sources, this article intends to show how American Jewish women on court actively shaped the sporting culture for both Jewish and non-Jewish women and, in doing so, significantly advanced the popularity of women's tennis in the 1920s, 1930s and beyond.

THE GROWTH OF TENNIS FOR AMERICAN JEWISH WOMEN

Tennis in the United States gained popularity initially as a lawn competition for the white Anglo-Saxon, Protestant upper classes as part of their elitist display of leisure and social status. At the country clubs that were largely their exclusive domain, tennis formed part of the social class distinction for those who had sufficient leisure time for sports. Tennis at the Newport Casino in Rhode Island, for example, formed part of the playground of the rich in New England along with other sports such as golf, polo, archery, swimming, and social activities such as dining and dancing. Lawn tennis was introduced to American white upper class sportsmen and sportswomen by Mary Ewing Outerbridge, who brought the game to members of the Staten Island Baseball and Cricket Club in 1874. Her brother and others soon became interested in lawn tennis, and this led to the first lawn tennis tournament in the United States on September 1, 1880. The United States National Lawn Tennis Association was formed in May 1881 and women's tennis soon followed with a national tournament, the United States Tennis Championship, beginning in 1889 (Gems, Borish and Pfister; Gillmeister; Tingay). Upper class Jewish women in the late nineteenth century, especially those of German Jewish descent, were allowed to participate at some of these tennis clubs (Borish, "Jewish American Women"). Tennis, like golf, offered upper-crust Jewish women a sport they could play competitively, most notably if they possessed outstanding abilities. Other Jewish women, particularly immigrants, generally first learned tennis at Young Men's-Young Women's Hebrew Associations (YMHA/YWHA), known as Jewish Y's in the early twentieth century. Eventually, by the inter-war period, some American Jewish women sufficiently excelled in tennis to move from exclusive clubs to the competitive public arena.

Most notably, in the early decades of the twentieth century, the New York YWHA, which opened in 1903, accommodated the activities of Jewish sportswomen. A new women's Y featured "a swimming pool, 20 feet by 60 feet, a gymnasium" and "a roof garden with tennis courts." One New York newspaper hailed the Association as "the most comprehensive program of physical education in the country for Jewish women and girls" (Borish, "'Athletic Activities of Various Kinds'" 248–49; Borish, "'An Interest in Physical Well-Being'"). Likewise, in Hartford, Connecticut, the YWHA was founded in 1915 by a group of Jewish young women, originally in the facilities of the city's YMHA. The association grew fairly quickly, and the YWHA leaders decided they needed a place for their own activities, rather than face constraints on religious, educational, and sporting endeavors. By 1919, Hartford YWHA members took physical education classes and played sports like swimming, tennis, basketball, volleyball, badminton, track-and-field, and bowling; and some young women competed in leagues against both Jews and non-Jews. Although the Athletic Department lacked sufficient facilities, Hartford Jewish women pursued sports using public high school gymnasiums, public parks, the Young Women's Christian Association (YWCA) swimming pools, and other places for their athletics including tennis. The Hartford YWHA team played the YWCA in tennis, bowling, and other sports. The women also pursued tennis competitions, using the public courts in Hartford. Jewish girls, wanting to learn tennis, received free lessons from the chair of athletics, who organized this activity with the support of her administrative committee. While these institutional activities illustrated the growing popularity of tennis for some Jewish women on the local level, the American and American Jewish press focused, as they did in other sports, on the national stars of the day. And during the inter-war period, Jewish female tennis players succeeded in tournaments to a remarkable extent and were accordingly singled out and hailed by the press.

CLARA GREENSPAN AND THE GENDERING OF WOMEN'S TENNIS

Within the competitive ranks of women's tennis, a fair number of Jewish star players emerged in the early twentieth century. Clara Greenspan became one of the most prominent female tennis players, earning accolades as a champion in the late 1920s. Greenspan, the captain, coach, and manager of the Hunter College tennis team, won the Women's New York State Singles and Doubles Championships and Eastern Clay Court Championship in 1928. Greenspan also played in the National Tennis Championships at Forest Hills, and the following year, she won the Women's Metropolitan Clay Court Championship and was a finalist at the prestigious North-South women's singles tournament, where she also made it to the finals in the doubles event. Highpoints in Greenspan's tennis career include her selection to participate in the popular team matches for the Sears Cup, representing the Eastern Lawn Tennis Association, competing against the top players of the New England Lawn Tennis Association. Her success brought media attention, as mainstream newspapers such as the *New York Times* as well as Jewish papers covered her tennis achievements and male journalists often resorted to somewhat gendered language to emphasize the feminine aspects of her achievements as a Jewish athlete.

In 1928, as Greenspan won victories on the court, *New York Times* sportswriter and journalist on women's tennis, Allison (Al) Danzig wrote about this emerging star. The headline on June 14, 1928 read, "Miss Francis Loses to Miss Greenspan. Tenth Ranking Player Put Out of Met. Clay Court Event, 4–6, 6–3, 6–2." Danzig noted, "Two young tennis players, one of them enjoying an established reputation on the courts and holding a position in the first ten, the other just beginning to make a name for herself in the game, met in the women's metropolitan clay court championship at the University Heights Tennis Club yesterday, and the verdict was victory for the newcomer." Danzig observed Greenspan's improvement during the match, which proved to be the decisive edge in the victory over her highly ranked opponent. According to Danzig, the left-handed Greenspan honed her shot making skills as the match progressed.

"It was also apparent that Miss Greenspan had a backhand drive, which never came back twice in the same direction, and always with good depth, whether it was played down the line or across court, and once she found the range of the lines with it the Jersey girl's [Francis'] problem was not going to be so simple" (35). The *New York Times* covered other Greenspan victories during 1928, as she won the Ardsley Tennis Clubs invitation tennis tournament, again beating Francis in a three set match, 2–6, 6–3, 6–4. Greenspan's power undermined stereotypes that Jews—let alone Jewish women—were physically inferior, and this theme was emphasized as a highlight in the reporting of the match: "The slight Miss Francis was unable to withstand the long rallies that featured nearly every game. The match was a base-line duel at first, but Miss Greenspan took the net more frequently as the match progressed and earned many points." The reporter noted how Francis "tired rapidly after the first set" (Danzig, "Miss Greenspan Wins Ardsley Tennis Final" 17). As Greenspan gained more victories with increased experience on the tennis court, Danzig applauded Greenspan's athletic ability: "The endurance of youth and the daring and sharpness of her ground strokes carried Miss Clara Greenspan to the women's metropolitan clay court championship yesterday, just as they earned for her the New York State and Eastern titles in 1928." Focusing on the female form in his gendered comments on Greenspan, however, Danzig also commented that, "the slender, dark-haired Hunter College girl outlasted Mrs. Bernard F. Stenz in a hard-fought match that consumed more than an hour in the broiling sun, to win at 6-3-9-7" (Danzig, "Met Tennis Crow to Miss Greenspan" S1).

The fact that some American Jewish women (like Greenspan) gained access to suitable gender-oriented American sports like tennis in college also caught the attention of American Jewish journalists. For example, Harry Conzel in "Our Sporting Column" of Pittsburgh's *Jewish Criterion* (April 1925) included material about the "American-Jewish Girl Athlete." He commented that, contrary to some popular perceptions that there was a lack of American female athletes, Jewish girls should also be factored into the growing popularity of sports for American girls in the 1920s. Indeed, that decade is often referred to as "The Golden Age of Sport," with "Golden People" as popular heroes, as sports gained increasing coverage in the print media and further wide dissemination thanks to the new technological advances of the radio. In various ways and for several diverse girls in American culture, sports became a more visible activity (Gems, Borish, and Pfister; Gallico). As American girls pursued certain physical activities, Conzel argued, "We thus find the American Jewish girl is by far the best conditioned, healthiest specimen of Jewish womanhood throughout the world." Part of this partaking of sport and physical culture activities for Jewish young women came from their expanded opportunities for sports at Jewish organizations like Jewish Y's and at other educational institutions. But there were in fact a variety of opportunities for Jewish women, as Conzel asserted:

> The Jewish girl in American has been affected by the athletic atmosphere which is prevalent in our schools and colleges—and true of our American life in general. In the last few years, this Jewish girl, taking full advantage of all these opportunities, has come to the forefront in tennis, swimming and basketball. ("Our Sporting Column" 44)

Some Jewish young women who were learning tennis at various YWHAs may have sought to emulate Greenspan as her exploits were highlighted in the American Jewish press. In August 1928, the *American Hebrew* featured Greenspan in a piece entitled "A Rising Star, Clara Greenspan, Winner of Many Championships," in which the male journalist praised her for displaying the "fine complexion that comes with a healthy outdoor life." Endorsing tennis for women, the *American Hebrew* writer pronounced that she "makes a picture equally attractive on the court or in a ballroom" (Gumpert; Levine, *Ellis Island to Ebbets Field* 204).

While such gendered comments about Greenspan's appearance undervalued her athleticism, other male journalists in the American Jewish press focused on their hope and expectation that she would maintain her tennis success. In particular, sports columnist George Joel often commented on Greenspan and other American Jewish sportswomen in his column "Jewish Sports Notes," published in *The Jewish Criterion*, *The Sentinel*, the *American Jewish Weekly* of Chicago and other newspapers during the 1920s and 1930s. Writing in the *Jewish Criterion* on June 22, 1928, Joel remarked, "Clara Greenspan, a Jewish young lady, won the Eastern Clay Court Championship when she defeated another Jewess, Florence Sheldon in the final round by the score of 6–2, 9–7." In this match, Sheldon lost because "Clara could outdrive and outplace her" (23). Unlike some of the other American Jewish tennis players who achieved success on court, discussed below, Greenspan did not come from a wealthy background and remained a student for most of her playing career. Joel remarked in *The Criterion* on June 29, 1928 after Greenspan was absent from some tennis tournaments that, "This column's favorite Jewish woman tennis star, Miss Greenspan, is on a forced vacation from tournament play. Not being one of the idle rich, she cannot afford to travel around the country to tournaments and has as yet not found a backer" (Joel, "Jewish Sport Notes" 27). Providing information to Jewish readers about Greenspan became a frequent element in Joel's sports reporting. He wrote, for example, in "Sport Notes," for July 20, 1928, "I am still very much interested in the progress of Clara Greenspan on the courts. The last month has been an idle one for the Jewish player, but she expects to play a few tournaments in August." He offered that, "I am willing to bet that she is going to raise havic [sic] with some of our ranking women tennis stars" (27).

Toward the end of the women's outdoor tennis season in 1928, Joel once again seemed optimistic about Greenspan's tennis career and her role as an American Jewish sportswoman. Referring to a match covered in the *New York Times*, he stated in *The Criterion* of October 5, 1928, "The outdoor tennis season is fast drawing to a cold close, but before the snow covers the courts Clara Greenspan managed to get in one more victory and clinch a national ranking, when she won the Ardsley Club Women's Tournament. . . . Miss Francis rated tenth last year, and I don't see how Miss Greenspan can be kept out of the ranking." Joel extolled Greenspan's athletic record on court:

> During the season Miss Greenspan won the Metropolitan, the New York State and the New Jersey State championships. All major tournaments with large entry lists. This is Clara's first year of big time tennis, as she began to attract attention only a few years ago, when she won the Girls' championship at Central Park, New York City. Her exploits this season definitely place her in the ranks of the stars, and I think that she has both the ability and the fight to go a good deal higher. The will to win is exceedingly important in tennis, and very few women players have it. They become easily frightened at their opponent's reputation and go to pieces. Miss Greenspan is a very hard young lady to impress, and especially so when another young lady is across the net. (40)

The following year, the American Jewish press, and especially Joel, continued to focus its attention on Greenspan's tennis career. In his "Jewish Sports Notes" column" in *The Sentinel* he covered Greenspan's victory on court in another tournament and stated, "Clara Greenspan Wins her First 1929 Title." In June, Joel declared, "Clara Greenspan, our one and only Jewish woman player, came through to win the Metropolitan Singles Championship by defeating Mrs. Stone in the final round in straight sets." Joel expounded Greenspan's tennis and Jewish identity in his comments:

> The Jewish girl was in rare form and blasted her opponent off the court with her forceful and clever placements. It was a sweet match to watch, plenty of action and very good tennis. It showed Clara a much improved player over her 1928 form when she won the New York State and Eastern titles to get an eleven ranking. Clara hopes to crash the first ten this year. I think she will. (13)

It is worth noting that, Greenspan received recognition from Joel as "our . . . Jewish" tennis player, showing the ethnic pride and Jewish identity linked with such a skilled female tennis player. While another Jewish tennis player, Helen Hull Jacobs, featured below, was just then emerging from success at the junior ranks and soon would show her athleticism in the senior ranks in tennis tournaments, Greenspan was still at this time "our one and only" top Jewish star. But she would not be so for long. Joel wrote that, "Helen Jacobs, of California, last year's Girl Champion of the United States is playing fine tennis. She ought to repeat last year's performance and besides make a high mark in the senior events" (Joel, *Jewish Criterion*, July 16, 1926, 31). Still, in the meantime, Joel continued to extoll Greenspan talents. In another of his "Jewish Sports Notes" columns, appearing in *The Sentinel*. he contended that, "Clara Greenspan, our Jewish tennis star, is conspicuous by her inactivity on the courts this spring. I haven't seen her name in a headline since spring when she was eliminated from a southern tournament" (Joel, June 7, 1929, 13). Moreover, a week later, Joel offered an explanation for Greenspan's lack of presence on the tennis court for certain competitions. "The Eastern Women's Singles Championship, which was won by Clara Greenspan last year, is being played without Clara's aid this year." Joel observed that she was not competing in this tournament this year because "She is practicing for the Sears Cup matches. She is a member of the team that will represent New York City" (Joel, June 14, 1929, 13).

The prestigious honor of being a member of the Sears Cup Team put Greenspan in the midst of the best amateur women tennis players in her region and the nation. The Sears Cup competition in June 1929 took place in Boston at the Longwood Cricket Club. "Boston Women Win Sears Cup, 6 to 4," the *New York Times* declared. "Boston captured three singles and two doubles matches to win the trophy for the third year in succession" (S2). The American Jewish press took pride in identifying one of the New York singles victors as Greenspan. Joel exclaimed that, "Clara Greenspan, number 11 on the women's singles list, was chosen as a member of the New York team that played the Boston team in Sears Cup matches at Boston." The New York women lost, he explained, "but through no fault of Clara's, who accounted for one point with a win against Mrs. H.

R. Guild in straight sets" ("Jewish Sports Notes, June 21, 1929, 44). Greenspan would continue her brilliant tennis career into the 1930s, but she was not the only outstanding American Jewish woman on the tennis court during the decade.

OTHER AMERICAN JEWISH WOMEN TENNIS PLAYERS AND SPORTING EXPERIENCES

In 1931, several American Jewish women joined Greenspan as teammates on the Sears Cup team, competing for the Eastern Lawn Tennis Association versus the New England Association and Middle Atlantic Association teams. These players included Millicent Hirsch, Baroness Levi, and Norma Taubele. The tennis matches for the Sears Cup took place at the Westchester Country Club in Rye, NY, one of the few elite Jewish country clubs in the area ("Nine Women Tennis Players" 40; Levine, "'Our Crowd at Play'" 172). Several of these American Jewish young women earned the attention of the American Jewish press during the 1930s. While Helen Jacobs, who will be discussed later in the article, excelled in international tournaments at this time, on the home front players like Baroness Giacomo Levi (formerly Maud Rosenbaum before her marriage to the Baron; later often identified by her second husband's name, after divorcing the Baron in 1934 and marrying H. Walter Blumenthal the following year) earned their own victories.

In 1934, Martha Neumark featured the Baroness in the *Jewish Criterion* and explained that while she "did not get to the finals, she gave clear indication of her superiority in a smashing defeat of Betty Nuthall, the British champion." Baroness Levi had a long career in tennis as "Chicagoans will remember this firmly-built, dark-complected [sic] thoroughbred as Maud Rosenbaum, daughter of the shoe magnate, whose life has been a continuous success of athletic conquests" and since "her divorce (to the Baron) she has been a familiar figure in the American sport world" (28). Others placed Levi's career in the context of the "two Helens," who will be discussed in the next section. "Whenever Helen Wills and Helen Jacobs go to Europe Baroness Giacomo Levi plays phenomenal tennis in this country, cleaning up one tournament after another. Baroness Giacomo Levi looks so Jewish that the ladies who enjoy meeting a real baroness explain: 'She is a perfect Italian type'" (Biron, "Strictly Confidential," May 13, 1932, 24). In previewing the US women's tennis championships in 1935 one journalist noted that beside Jacobs, "There will be three women tennis stars entered . . .Who are Jewish. . . .They are Mrs. Blumenthal (the former Baroness Giacomo Levi), Bonnie Miller and Millicent Hirsch" (Weiner, "The Sports World," August 30, 1935, 12).

In 1935, the *Jewish Exponent*, published in Philadelphia, featured a column "Womankind" by Emma Brylawski, who devoted an article to "Jewish Women in Sports." Brylawski singled out Baroness Levi, noting that she was the "ranking woman tennis player of the East for the past four years, and holder of about fifteen titles of importance." Brylawski added that Levi "first gained international acclaim when she overwhelmingly captured the five leading tennis tournaments held along the East coast, in 1932," propelling her to a top ten standing in the United States. Stressing her gender-role as a mother and the importance of this in her family life as wife of Baron Levi, an Italian Jew, Brylawski praised the baroness for interrupting her tennis competition for a time due to the illness of her daughter. Brylawski praised Levi as "one of the outstanding tennis players in America, and by far the most prominent Jewish woman tennis ace in the world, [who] sacrificed her chances to win one of the most important tournaments in the country in order to be at the beside of her sick daughter" (5). Later, Baroness Levi would return to the tennis courts to compete. Similarly, the *American Hebrew* discussed Baroness Levi and Millicent Hirsch, who earned a number four ranking in the US in 1934 (138). In 1935, the former Baroness Levi (now using the name of her second husband, Blumenthal) defeated fellow Jewish player Norma Taubele at the New York State Singles Championship in 1935. The following year. Taubele defeated Blumenthal in the 1936 finals.

Taubele rose through the junior ranks of tennis to later make her mark on the women's tennis scene. At times, she played with her mother in women's doubles events. The *New York Times* indicated, "Miss Taubele Wins with Mother's Aid" in a tournament in 1927. "Mrs. Rose Taubele and daughter, Miss Norma of New York, advanced to the final round of the women's doubles of the Eastern clay court tennis championship. The victory of the New York pair was unexpected." Taubele competed in some of the same tournaments as Clara Greenspan, as a 1929 *New York Times* article informed its readers. Journalist Grover Theis spotlighted Taubele with the headline, "Miss Norma Taubele is Tennis Victor," and described her athleticism in glowing terms:

> Particularly flaming was Miss Norma Taubele, who is red-haired and left-handed, when she maintained her pace as manifested during the waning season and defeated Miss Beatrice Moore in a fourth round match, 5–7, 6–2, 11–9, in the most strenuously contested match of

> the present tournament. Subsequently she paired with her sister, Elsa, also red-haired, to proceed through the second round of the doubles... (Theis 36)

As one might expect, players such as Taubele and Levi received special recognition from the American Jewish press for their athleticism on the court. Reviewing "The Sport Year" in 1934, journalist Haskell Cohen noted that even though star Helen Jacobs, "national women's champ, suffered unexpected defeat twice... Baroness Maud Levi, Mrs. Caroline Hirsch and Millicent Hirsch retained their high rankings, the latter winning the national girls' indoor title" (Cohen 179). Writing about "Jews in the Nation's Sports," journalist Conzel included women tennis players. In the tennis rankings, behind top-ranked Helen Jacobs in the women's national singles standing at the fourth rating "was Mrs. H. Walter Blumenthal, the former Baroness Maud Levi, who won the eastern clay court tennis crown, the New York state women's clay court singles titles and the Women's New Jersey singles championships." Joining Levi/Blumenthal in high standing were doubles teammates "Miss Millicent Hirsh of New York, former national girls' singles champion," and Taubele ("Jews in the Nation's Sports" 161). In 1935 the United States Lawn Tennis Association had Helen Jacobs "ranked number one among women's tennis player and Mrs. H. W. Blumenthal is placed 11th" ("Jews Gain High National Rankings in Tennis" 7). Vying for top tennis honors in 1936 with Jacobs was Taubele, who "won the New York State singles, the Eastern clay court singles, and with Miss Grace Surber, also a Jewess, captured the New York State doubles, Eastern clay court doubles, and the New Jersey doubles" (Conzel, "Parade of Jewish Champions" 87).

At times, Jewish tennis players, similar to their golf counterparts, faced discrimination in the sport. Levi/Blumenthal claimed such bias in the US Lawn Tennis Association national title tournament in 1936. Charging "deliberate prejudice and discrimination," she filed a complaint against the tennis committee "as the result of the committee's failure to place her in the seeded list of the women's national tennis champions at Forest Hills." The seeding committee matched Levi/Blumenthal, ranked at the time fifth in the country, against the Helen Jacobs in the first round, although her tennis record and standing merited an easier first round opponent. Blumenthal lost to Jacobs in a tough match, 6–3, 6–4 ("Charges Bias" 8; "Norma Taubele Wins N.Y Women's Tennis Title" 8, quoted in Borish, "Jewish Sportswomen" 95).

During the 1930s Jewish women tennis players in America continued to display their skills. Even at the highest competitive level such as the United States Women's Tennis Championships, American Jewish women became part of the highly capable women players competing for laurels. In 1939, a journalist explained, "Norma Taubele, Grace Surber, Millicent Hirsch and Frances Longman comprise a feminine quarter that has earned more than its share of glory. Although none holds a national title, among them they share some twenty-seven junior and women's divisional championships" (Weiner, "Jewish Athletes Prove Noble Sportsmen" 121).

Some of these American Jewish tennis players continued their athletic triumph on the court. Young tennis prodigy Millicent Hirsch was singled out by the *New York Times*: "Outplaying her older opponent at every stage, 13-year old Millicent Hirsch of the Bronx easily defeated Miss Vivian Wunderlich 6-3, 6-2" to win the Manhattan junior girl's singles tennis championship. Hirsch teamed up with her doubles partner to earn the doubles tennis crown, as well ("Net Title to Miss Hirsch" 26). In another tennis tournament featuring young Jewish women players in this summer of 1930, Hirsch outplayed her older Jewish opponent Miss Grace Surber. "Playing an all-around game of unusual polish and astuteness," the *New York Times* praised Hirsch's tennis strategy. "[The] 13-year old New York girl, scored a surprising victory over Miss Grace Surber of Jackson Heights, the top seeded player to reach the finals of the junior girls' centre tournament of the Eastern Lawn Tennis Association. The hard fought victory by Hirsch was earned by the score of 4-6, 6-1, 6-4" ("Miss Surber Loses in Tennis Upset" 22).

When playing some of the senior Jewish women players Hirsch did not always play victorious tennis. Nonetheless, tennis reporter Danzig praised her in one match by noting, "The compact, gracefully executed strokes of Miss Norma Taubele were pitted against the varied repertoire and stylish backhand of one of the leading junior players in the metropolitan area yesterday in the women's New York State Championship at the Jackson Heights Tennis Club." In this tennis event, "All other activity on the court was of secondary interest to the gallery as the 16-year old Millicent Hirsh [sic] of Evander Childs High School fought her way to the front in the first set against Miss Taubele." In three sets, 4-6, 6-1, 6-3, Taubele defeated Hirsch, "by virtue of her greater experience and lasting powers" (Danzig, "Miss Francis Loses to Miss Greenspan" 23). In the next few years these Jewish women tennis players continued matching their athletic capabilities with all comers, making the "Honor Roll of Jews in Sports—[Jewish Year] 5696" including "Mrs. Maud Blumenthal, Miss Norma Taubele, Grace Surber, Millicent Hirsch" (20). These increasing numbers of female tennis players were celebrated in the Jewish press, but of all the American

Jewish women who found success on the courts during the inter-war period, one stood above the rest: Helen Hull Jacobs.

HELEN HULL JACOBS AND THE GOLDEN AGE OF TENNIS

Certainly the most renowned Jewish female tennis players of the inter-war period was Helen Hull Jacobs, who won five grand slam titles and was the top ranked women's player in the world in 1936. Jacobs distinguished herself by being a leading advocate for dress reform in tennis during her time as a top player, and she was also one half of a major rivalry in women's tennis with Helen Wills (Moody) in the late 1920s and 1930s. This intense tennis rivalry, discussed below, helped shape the discourse surrounding American women tennis players on the tennis courts—both Jewish and non-Jewish. In fact, Jacobs, in the eyes of the American Jewish press, became known as "our own Helen Jacobs" or more simply, "our Helen," as compared with "Queen Helen" or "Helen the first," as Helen Wills was often described. In contrast, the mainstream American press sometimes referred to Jacobs as "Helen the second" and Wills as "Our Helen" due to Wills' numerous championships and victories over Jacobs. As historian of women's tennis Larry Engelmann explained, by 1925, "The press was already referring to Jacobs as 'Little Helen' and Wills now as 'Big Helen'. Jacobs was following in the footsteps of Wills, practicing with Pop Fuller [Wills' former coach William Fuller] and taking careful instruction from Hazel Wightman," a leading figure in women's tennis and former champion (101; Gallico 170–71; Joel, January 28, 1927, 15; Messenger 14).

Jacobs was born August 6, 1908 in Globe, Arizona. Her father, Roland Jacobs, a mining executive of Miami Copper, was Jewish whereas her mother Eula Hull was not. At a young age, the family moved to the San Francisco area where her father became a newspaper advertising executive. He gave Helen her first tennis racket, and she started playing the sport at age thirteen. It was a sport her father, in failing health, could play with her. Jacobs later recollected, "He had two rackets, one of which he gave to me. In the evenings when he came home he and I would walk up to Lafayette Square and, [this is] where he taught me the rudiments of the game." After she beat her father one day, Jacobs explained, they agreed "that I might try my hand in the public park tournament" (Jacobs, *Beyond the Game* 16–17, 27, 35). Jacobs spent most of her childhood in Berkeley, California and her tennis career began in earnest there. In *Beyond the Game: An Autobiography*, she recalled:

> I expected to reinforce my success with experience and advice, for I had already been fortunate enough to attract the attention of a well-known figure in California tennis. As early as 1923 William Fuller was gaining widespread reputation as a tennis coach because of his work with Helen Wills. . . . This he did with Helen Wills to whom he threw balls by the boxful, and this he proposed to do with me. (41)

Jacobs played numerous tournaments in Berkeley, earning victories and learning from defeats. She joined the Berkeley Tennis Club as had Helen Wills before her. In 1924, Jacobs traveled with her mother to participate in the National Junior Championships. Jacobs affirmed, "The night that Mr. Fuller telephoned to tell me that I was to leave Berkeley August 7th I could have wept with relief. It infused my hopes and ambitions with reality" (Jacobs, *Beyond the Game* 53–54; Messenger 15). At the age of fifteen Jacobs made her Eastern tennis debut. By then, Wills was too old for junior tennis championships and Jacobs won consecutive junior national tennis titles in 1924 and 1925. Yet, even then, the "two Helens" were starting to become interrelated in the press and in their experiences.

When Jacobs moved from the junior championships to compete in the senior women's championships her career excelled and so did issues of her form and style on court. The "two Helens" rivalry filled pages of the mainstream American press as well as the American Jewish press. In 1927, *New York Times* sportswriter Danzig touted, "Net Fame Sought By Another Helen. Miss Jacobs Arrives Here from Coast and Starts Practice Matches." More than this, the journalist described "Two Careers Parallel. Both She and Miss Wills Live in Berkeley, Go to Same School and Same Club." Danzig informed readers how the two careers "offer a remarkable parallel." In addition to both living in Berkeley, "Miss Jacobs's family [is] now occupying the house formerly tenanted by the Wills family; both belong to the same tennis club; both attend the same private school, both have won the national junior girls' championship twice"; furthermore in the fall, "Miss Jacobs will follow further in the footsteps of her more famous illustrious namesake by matriculating at the University of California" (10). Jacobs revealed at this time, "From the standpoint of tennis as a personal career, 1927 was a year of the greatest importance. I had had a full season of competition in women's tennis" (Jacobs, *Beyond the Game* 89).

Ten years after that all important year of 1927, Jewish journalist Morris Weiner recalled Jacobs' role on the women's tennis circuit in his "Sports Outlook" column in *American Jewish Outlook*. Weiner recalled, "Ever since that day ten years ago in 1927 when as a shy nineteen-year-old-girl she first came out of the West, Helen Jacobs has been a dominant figure on the tennis courts of America and the continent". Weiner further opined, "And, if consistency is the hallmark of the genuine champion, then Miss Jacobs, who derives her Jewishness from her father (who died recently), is a reigning queen in the fullest sense of the expression." He explained that her triumphs at various tennis contests placed her among the greatest women's tennis players during the golden age in the 1920s and 1930s:

> Of all the women who have played tennis in the half century that they have been granted championship recognition, four alone have commanded universal attention usually reserved for men athletes. Dynamic Suzanne Lenglen, the French Pavlowa of the courts was one. The brilliant Molla Mallory was another. Poker faced Helen Wills Moody and Helen Jacobs are the other two . . . And, if not for the fact that she [Jacobs] was a contemporary of the great Helen Wills, she would have sat in triumph in all the throne rooms of tennis long ago. ("Sports Outlook" 16)

Weiner highlighted the various top women tennis players against whom Jacobs competed, and noted again the place of rival Helen Wills. "The Jewish girl made her debut in tournament tennis in 1926, at a time when competition among American women never was keener. Miss Helen Wills, fresh from a triumph over the glamorous Lenglen, ruled despotically and showed not the slightest inclination of relaxing her grip on her titles. Mrs. Mallory, a top-notcher for a decade still possessed the inherent class which carried her to the national championship that year, eleven years after her first victory" (Weiner, "Sports Outlook" 16). Despite the presence of such amazing female tennis players, Jacobs, indeed, gained impressive victories on court. She won the United States National Championships in Singles from 1932 to 1935, won the United States Women's Doubles Championship in 1932, and 1934–35, the Mixed Doubles Champion in 1934, and earned the prestigious Wimbledon Ladies Championship in 1936. Jacobs also represented the US in women's international tennis competitions on the Wightman Cup as a Team Member in 1927–37 and 1939. Yet, despite these triumphs, the popular focus of the public on her career always seemed to come back to the rivalry with Helen Wills.

The spotlight on Jacobs' rivalry with Wills shaped the commentary in the American mainstream and American Jewish press throughout her career. Being an American Jewish female athlete, as Joel asserted, "Our Helen was National Girls' Champion a few years back, and she has developed into a well rounded player. A few more years of experience and she'll beat anybody in the East" ("Jewish Sports Notes," January 28, 1927, 15). In fact, Joel praised Jacobs' talent on court as she moved into the senior ranks of women's competitive tennis. He remarked about this 1927 national tennis championship, "only one Jewish girl can be found among the entries. Of course it is Helen Jacobs, and she has won her way into the third round. Unfortunately," Joel explained, Helen "is in the same side of the draw with Helen Wills, and hence it is highly improbable that the Jewish girl will be a finalist" ("Jewish Sports Notes," September 2, 1927, 29). Jacobs, in becoming a national star, who, unlike some of the other American Jewish women, advanced beyond the New York and California state tournaments to reach the US women's national tournament and also played in international tournaments, quickly gained high praise. Joel ascertained earlier in 1928 that in the realm of Jews in sport, "In the women's list our own Helen Jacobs was ranked No. 1. Helen Wills is, of course, the best player on the West Coast, or any other coast for that matter, but due to her illness was not ranked this year. Our Helen was National Girls' Champion a few years back, and has developed into a well rounded player" ("Jewish Sports Notes," Jan. 28, 1927, 15). Noting the frequency of these tennis talents competing against each other over the years, one journalist in the *Jewish Criterion* offered that the similarity in their geographic and personal path in tennis should not be an overriding theme. "The mere fact that Both Mrs. [Wills] Moody [married to Frederick S. Moody and therefore often identified with her married surname] and Helen Jacobs hail from Berkeley, Cal.," the author declared, "is no reason for any one referring to them as a couple of Berkeley Belles," putting gendering terminology ahead of tennis skill ("Notes of Interest" 21).

The tennis matches between Jacobs and Wills (Moody) were dominated by Wills for most of the span of their rivalry. Their eighth match, in 1933, however, became one for the ages. As one writer described it, "The Jacobs-Wills rivalry was said to dominate women's tennis as complete as the rivalry between Queen Elizabeth and Mary Queen of Scots once dominated British politics. Jacobs and Wills met each other eight times, and seven times Wills walked away victorious." But in the eighth contest, "Wills simply walked off the court, defaulted the Forest Hills finals of 1933 to a startled and deeply disappointed Jacobs, 8–6, 3-6, 3-0" (Messenger 15; "Sport," *Newsweek* 18). Wills' withdrawal occurred after she claimed a back injury, and the controversial contest, which gave Jacobs her second of four US championship titles (she won her first in 1932 against Carolin Babcock), helps reveals how American Jewish periodicals viewed and understood "Our Helen" in the 1930s.

Helen Hull Jacobs, ca. 1935. Courtesy of the International Tennis Hall of Fame and Museum, Newport, RI.

THE "TWO HELENS" AND POPULAR PERCEPTIONS OF WOMEN TENNIS STARS

As Helen Jacobs gained acclaim by winning tournaments and as Helen Wills continued to show her tennis prowess, the two remained linked in the tennis world. In the early years of the rivalry, as mentioned above, Jacobs was on the losing end of a number of matches to Wills, who, due to her cool and controlled demeanor on the court, was nicknamed "The Ice Queen" and "Little Miss Poker Face" as the press assigned different skills and personalities to the two tennis stars. According to renowned sportswriter Paul Gallico, Wills "had the reputation as well as appearance of being completely glacial, unemotional and implacable, and yet I, in the company of a few other sportswriters once saw an almost incredible Helen Wills with her hair down." Gallico lauded Wills as having "the courage of a lioness, the stoicism of an Indian brave, and the beauty of a Greek goddess" (168–69). Another journalist explained that, "Miss Wills made it unbearable by jealously guarding her laurels and acting condescendingly. In recent years, making her annual rankings, she has carefully rated Miss Jacobs obscurely. Miss Jacobs 'hated her "second fiddle" role'" ("Sport," *Newsweek* 18).

In contrast, some journalists described Jacobs' tennis style and demeanor as countering that of Wills. Noting she was a new player in the international competition of the US versus England in the Wightman Cup in 1927, Joel observed in the *Jewish Criterion*, "Helen Jacobs' first appearance as a member of the American team in the Wightman Cup Matches resulted in her defeat by sixteen year-old Betty Nuthall of England.... Miss Jacobs is still in the process of developing. She has the pace and strength for the game, but needs the seasoning that comes from constant campaigning." He further explained Jacobs' importance:

> There is only one star woman Jewish player in the country, but she makes up in quality what we lack in quantity. Helen Jacobs was a member of the American Wightman Cup team, and has a victory over Molla Mallory, the 1926 singles champion. Helen is sure of a ranking among the first five. Miss Jacobs is the first Jewish woman in America to gain a place in the tennis sun. ("The Year in Sports," September 19, 1927, 368)

Yet when Wills defeated Jacobs in the 1928 Women's National Single Championship at Forest Hills, Joel commented on Jacobs' defeat as well as her character, in contrast to Wills. "Our Helen was just not in Wills' class and I don't think she will be for a long time" after a 6–2, 6– loss. "On the other hand," Joel declared, "Helen Jacobs is a delight to watch. She makes wry faces, smiles at the good ones, gesticulates and chases a ball as though her life depended on it. She takes her tennis very seriously and when she loses a little crying in the club house is not unusual" ("Jewish Sports Notes," Sept. 7, 1928, 16A). Journalist Danzig hailed the victory of Wills as she soundly defeated Jacobs. "The most devastating power ever applied to a tennis ball by a woman ... carried Miss Helen Wills, twenty-three year-old Berkeley (Cal.) girl, to her fifth national championship yesterday, bringing to a close the campaign that has seen her win the premier laurels of tennis at Auteuil, Wimbledon, and Forest Hills without the loss of a set in three months of play" (Danzig, "Miss Wills Retains National Net Crown" 26). Sportswriter Westbrook Pegler in the *Chicago Daily*

Tribune announced, "Miss Wills Wins Battle of the Helens; Retains Title" (17). Thanks to this kind of journalistic rhetoric, the two Helens certainly became pitted in the press as well as on the tennis court.

In her own recollection of competing against the great women's champions, Jacobs wrote in *Gallery of Champions* (1949) on this first meeting with Wills in the national championship singles, "Although a recapitulation of the match showed that I earned more points than she, her errors were negligible in comparison with mine, as I overhit the lines in an effort to match her length." Jacobs explained that to play Wills "was to play a machine. There was little, if any conversation, no joviality, and to this the gallery reacted, becoming grim in its partnership." Of note, Jacobs admitted, "The press had long since confused incompatibility with the elements of a 'feud' in our matches, which became less agreeable to both of us as they inevitably occurred" (25–26). In short, the press deemed these Wills versus Jacobs tennis contests as a "cat fight" (Engelmann 339). Yet earlier in her tennis career, the press described Jacobs as "Speedy Afoot" and "Needs Competition to Develop Into a Great Star." A *Washington Post* article asked, "Will Helen Jacobs develop into an as great a tennis player as Helen Wills?" ("Miss Jacobs Is Speedy Afoot" 19). Her partner for the 1934 United States Mixed Doubles Championship, George Lott, commented that she "got the furthest with the leastest. [sic] To be exact, she had a forehand chop, a sound backhand, and lots and lots of stomach muscles" (Messenger 15).

The controversial match between Jacobs and Wills in the 1933 United States National Women's Singles Championship was played into the third set before Wills quit. A *Los Angeles Times* story summarized the way the championship match ended: "Mrs. Moody Defaults. Helen Jacobs Triumphs. Trailing by Three Games in the Third and Deciding Set, Net Queen Withdraws." Journalist Alan Gould quoted Wills on the match as offering, "'I Felt as if I Were Going to Faint', Says Star; Passes Up Doubles." Gould wrote in his coverage of this highly anticipated battle between Jacobs and Wills Moody, "Facing apparently certain defeat since 1926 in singles competition and on the verge of collapse, the result of wearing a back brace that troubled her right hip and leg. Mrs. Moody defaulted to Miss Jacobs after losing the first three games of the final set. The scores of the match that were hard fought and often brilliant, for two sets were 8–6, 3–6, 3–0, default." The 7,000 spectators watching the tennis match understandably were disappointed, but they "accorded an ovation to Miss Jacobs, who rose to her greatest heights by outplaying Mrs. Moody for the first time in her career and capturing the national championship for the second consecutive year" (Gould 1). Noting that Jacobs, who previously was "always merely 'Helen the Second,' deserved the full fruits of a gallantly won triumph. From the outset," Gould revealed that Jacobs "played with a determination and a resourcefulness that soon made it certain the seven-time former champion was in for a battle of her life, under any circumstance" (Gould, 1, Pt. 4).

Newsweek magazine recorded the momentous match with the tennis headline: "Mrs. Moody Quits Game in Dramatic Default." In this amazing sports moment, *Newsweek* reported that Wills/Moody did not faint; "Instead she picked up her famous blue sweater, told the umpire. Ben Wright, her legs wouldn't work, defaulted, and slowly left the stadium. Thus Miss Jacobs herself reported to be suffering from heart trouble became the new 'Queen' of tennis." The thousands of spectators believed Wills Moody should have played out the "final set even if she just let the balls whiz by. Some said that Mrs. [Wills] Moody, near defeat for the first time since 1926, had forgotten how to lose graciously." Furthermore, observers offered, "Those who termed Mrs. Moody's conduct 'inexcusable' explained it by recalling the feud that has long existed between the two California Helens" ("Sport," *Newsweek* 18).

Prior to this famed match, Jacobs recalled that she incurred an injury during the 1933 tennis season and that this might adversely affect her play in pursuit of the US National women's tennis title. After Jacobs's quarter-final match her doctor began "to pray for rain. I had aggravated the debilitating trouble in my side at Wimbledon and Seabright [tennis tournaments], where I played in heavy rain, and I needed a rest before my semi-final round against Dorothy Round." Jacobs acknowledged, "The drastic measures suggested by a specialist in Boston were not feasible until the tournament was over. Rest did not seem possible until it began to rain the morning of my scheduled match against Dorothy." The delay of matches helped Jacobs improve her health. "The five days respite were a joy to me." She recollected, "Noah could not have been happier to see the sun than I was when it finally reappeared." Jacobs, now rested and ready to play Dorothy Round was also "eager ... to play Helen Moody" in the finals, as the winner of this semi-final match would gain the opportunity to do (Jacobs, *Beyond the Game* 166–67).

Jacobs triumphed in her match against Round to play in the final she won by default over Helen Wills Moody. In later years, sports writer Gallico discussed the contentious finish to the match and recalled that another Golden Age of Tennis star, "Big Bill" Tilden, stated that, "when Mrs. Moody [Wills] defaulted, Helen Jacobs, meeting her at the umpires stand ... put her hand on her shoulder and said—'Won't you rest a minute, Helen?' Miss Wills coldly replied, 'Take your hand off my shoulder', picked up her racquets and left the court"

(Gallico 175). On the default by her rival, Jacobs explained, "'Mrs. Moody Did Right.'" She refuted the claims of the "cat fight" between the two tennis rivals. "Dissipating reports that of a personal feud with Mrs. Moody, Miss Jacobs emphatically said regarding her opponent and fellow Californian: 'I do like her. Because you are not a very great friend of some one [sic] it doesn't necessarily follow that you are not friendly'" (25).

HELEN HULL JACOBS AND HER INFLUENCE ON TENNIS

In the 1930s, especially following her victory over Wills in 1933, Jacobs received plaudits in the American press. She was named the Associated Press "Outstanding Woman Performer" in 1933 and in a headline about the voting, the *Atlanta Constitution* stated, "Helen Jacobs Leads Women Athletic Stars. Tennis Champion Voted Best" (see also "Helen Jacobs Tops Nation's Athletic Poll). The article noted that she surpassed women's national golf champion Virginia Van Wie, and the Associated Press sports poll named this "former crown princess of tennis as the queen of sports for 1933" (10). The American Jewish press proudly reported on Jacobs' success as well in 1934, when she "has been listed as American's No. 1 racquet woman and had the pleasure of turning down an offer of $20,000 to turn professional," in order to remain an amateur and compete in women's tournaments (Biron, "Strictly Confidential," January 13, 1935, 14).

In 1935, a full column for "Who's Who in Women's Tennis" in the *Chicago Tribune* was devoted to Jacobs and included a recent defeat in another closely contested match with Wills at Wimbledon. The column reported that Jacobs missed winning the famed Wimbledon championship "by an inch." In this match, "after an exchange of shots Miss Jacobs leaped into the air and hit a well placed over-head smash which would have swept her opponent from the court, but luck intervened, the ball hit the top of the net, and bounded back into the court." In assessing this title match between the two Helens, the reporter informed readers, "To lose by an inch of winning the most coveted tennis title in all the world would have caused the average contender many a heartache, but Miss Jacobs met it with a smile" ("Who's Who in Women's Tennis" 18). In an American Jewish periodical the match also received attention. In "Jews in the Nation's Sports," columnist Conzel declared, "Among Jewish women players Helen Jacobs, of course, dominated the field. Although she lost to her arch-rival Mrs. Helen Wills Moody, in the finals of the all-England women's singles tennis champions when the latter made a last minute rally, Miss Jacobs," Conzel pointed out, "went on to retain her American national singles title" ("Jews in the Nation's Sports" 98). On her loss to Wills Moody, Jacobs revealed, "It was useless after the match to wonder what I should have done, and all-important to put it out of my mind and concentrate on the American season" (Jacobs, *Beyond the Game* 264). Although she did not win Wimbledon in 1935, Jacobs was awarded an honorary membership to the Wimbledon England Tennis Club, the first time a non-Wimbledon champion had gained this honor ("Honors Helen Jacobs" 2).

The following year, Jacobs finally triumphed at Wimbledon. Winning the tournament "after 8 years of trying," gave Jacobs great pride as she "succeeded to the title of Mrs. Helen Wills Moody on the Wimbledon greens this afternoon after a dogged tooth and nail battle." Significantly, in a time of Nazi ascendancy and in the same year as the Berlin Olympics, she defeated Hilda Sperling of Denmark, born in Germany, 6-2, 4-6, 7-5, yet residing in Denmark. In her victory, Jacobs, "a strong, attractive figure in shorts, on the green courts, kept the Wimbledon title in the American family" ("Helen Jacobs Wins English Tennis Crown" A9).

Time magazine featured Jacobs on the cover for September 14, 1936. The cover caption read "Helen Hull Jacobs. Where there Isn't a Wills, there's a way . . . " The caption again referred to the longstanding rivalry between these two Helens as "The rivalry between these two girls [that] grew from the courts to the newspapers." Moreover, the article continued, "This year Helen Wills Moody was not in the tournament and Helen Jacobs at last found her way to her first Wimbledon title." In the same article, *Time* remarked, "As No.1 tennist, Helen Jacobs has a game marked less by brilliance of speed or stroke than by steadiness and tactical skill. Her most dependable stroke is a forehand slice, taught her by Tilden" ("Sport," *Time* cover and 36–45).

After the unnamed author continued describing other of her qualities on the court, he then felt further constrained to note that "Helen Jacobs is not a Jew" ("Sport," *Time* cover, 38, 40). It is unclear why the author felt the need to put this in, although, strictly speaking, he might be said to have a point. That is, if one were to define her identity in accordance with longstanding rabbinical tradition, then one could argue that, since she was not born of a Jewish mother, she was not Jewish from the perspective of more orthodox traditions. But since one of the hallmarks of modern Jewish identity is the right to choose one's identity, and Jacobs became identified as Jewish and apparently also identified herself as Jewish, the writer's qualification may have been motivated more by anti-Semitism, reflecting a desire not to allow this tennis champion the right to be identified as having a specifically Jewish heritage. In contrast, such attitudes and statements may have been why the American Jewish press preferred to ignore such technicalities and so eagerly accepted Jacobs as its "own" Helen.

Following her victory over Wills at the 1933 US Championship, a reporter from the *Jewish Criterion* lauded Jacobs' tennis victory but also wanted to reaffirm her Jewish identity. "We offer a five dollar book to anybody who will supply us with authoritative information on the Jewish-ness of Helen Jacobs, the tennis star." The reporter conveyed, "Personally we do believe that she is the daughter of a Jewish advertising man of California (Biron, "Strictly Confidential," September 15, 1933, 63). Three years later, American Jewish periodicals hailed Jacobs' victory at Wimbledon. In "Jewish Champions Hold Spotlight in Almost Every Field of Sport," Irv Kupcinet in the *Jewish Advocate*, asserted about tennis that, "No sport produced more Jewish champions last year. . . . Helen Jacobs reached her life's ambition when she finally won the Wimbledon title, defeating Hilda Sperling of Germany, 6–2, 4–6, 7–5. In doing so, Jacobs became "the best woman player of the world." He noted other American Jewish women stars in the sport of tennis such as Norma Taubele ("Jewish Champions Hold Spotlight" 25, 27, 29). In the "Jewish Sports Champions on Parade" piece in the *Jewish Advocate* the following year, once again Jacobs received accolades. Morris Weiner pronounced, "When speaking of tennis the name of Helen Jacobs still comes first for amateur honors in America, followed closely by Norma Taubele, Grace Surber, and Baroness Maude Levi" (Weiner, "Jewish Sports Champions on Parade" 27).

Another impact of Helen Hull Jacobs in tennis involves her activism in support of dress reform in the sport. Jacobs advocated for, and wore, shorts in tennis matches in the late 1920s and early 1930s, at a time when short skirts were just making their initial appearance in women tennis. Jacobs wrote about her quest to wear tennis clothing promoting freedom of movement on court in her chapter titled: "A 'Short' and Long Problem" in her autobiography, *Beyond the Game* (173–76). In 1929, the *New York Times* claimed, "U. S. Women Tennis Stars Plan to Adopt Stockingless Mode in Play at Wimbledon," and that year, Jacobs arrived at Wimbledon, and with a few other English players, declared "their intention of not being 'handicapped' by hose in this year's international competition at this famous English stadium." Specifically, Jacobs asserted, "This stocking business is merely a question of comfort and freedom on the courts." She continued, "In California this year nearly everybody played without stockings and it undoubtedly helps one's game. At Wimbledon I shall not wear stockings" (37). She seemed to have worn shorts only in practice, however, rather than an official match at the time. Four years later though, at the US National Women's Championships that she eventually won after Wills withdrew from the title match, Jacobs paved the way in women's tennis by wearing shorts. "Helen Jacobs Makes Debuts in 'Scanties'. National Tennis Champion Dons Shorts Today for First Time in Public Appearance." At this tournament, Jacobs planned her "debut in shorts. She's been wearing 'em in practice several days and tomorrow, if the sun shines, she will begin the defense of her title in the scantiest attire ever worn by a queen of American tennis." Jacobs asserted her right to wear the new tennis costume:

> They're really a tremendous advantage . . . . Nothing but prejudice has been preventing us for years. I know they improve my game and all the other girls say the same. I know I've lost many points through my racket catching in my skirt. Not only that, but they're cooler and enable one to get around so much faster, particularly in the latter stages of a hard match. (A9)

Male tennis officials did not publicly object to the new trends in tennis attire, and Jacobs donned the new tennis fashion at Wimbledon in 1934 following the advice of a male tennis player. "She achieved the goal of all young female notables by establishing a fashion in clothes. This was when Bunny [Henry] Austin advised her to play tennis in shorts," and she did so. Jacobs wore shorts "in the presence of Queen Mary at Wimbledon in 1934." Her tennis style gained publicity. "Her shorts, more becoming than the Wills' eyeshade and longer than those worn by most girl tennists, were made for her by a London men's tailor." *Time* magazine noted that Jacobs "still gets them from him, demands for fittings to a pair," not positively endorsing this pioneering tennis costume for women ("Sport," *Time* 40). A Jewish journalist highlighted the influence of Jacobs on other young women racket sport players during the 1936 period, a time of tension with Jews about participation in the Nazi Olympics. Irv Kupcinet in "The World of Sport," published in the Nashville *Observer,* praised her by noting, "It's not very often that a Jewish lassie causes any whoop-de-do on the athletic scene. Helen Hull Jacobs, the glorious girl from equally glorious California, is one, but aside from the wizard of the net, how many others are there?" (8).

As her career drew to a close, Jacobs played Wills once again in a tournament final, this time at Wimbledon in 1938. Jacobs was injured and lost the match easily. But contrary to her opponent's behavior in 1933, the press lauded what was perceived as Jacobs' sportsmanship and respect for the game. "Jacobs had torn the sheath of her Achilles tendon with the score tied 4–4 in the first set, but she refused to default. Hazel Wightman, tennis star of an earlier era, came down out of the stands to urge her to give up, but Jacobs insisted she wouldn't leave the court until the match was over" (Messenger 15).

Jacobs not only received coverage in the media, but she also became part of a book celebrating the exploits of various American Jewish women. In a review of *Little Women Grow Bold* (1936), authored by Mary Elizabeth Ford, the reviewer explained that the book covered the past accomplishments of women, including those who excelled in sport. The book portrayed "this record of bold and brave ladies of might and brawn" giving mention "to Helen Jacobs in tennis, Elaine Rosenthal in golf and Mrs. Oscar Straus in exploration. The best proof of the emergence of Jewish women in sports is the fact that so few women are mentioned in this book, which deals, mostly with has-beens," with the present period showing more American Jewish women participating in sports (Mann 15). Ford praised the tennis proficiency of Jacobs and once again identified the intense competition and rivalry between the "two Helens." The author expressed the sentiment that "more pronounced than ever" there was a "yearning for some new heroine to come forward and overpower the imperial Helen [Wills]." And in that feat Helen Jacobs showed her mettle. Reminding readers of the famous match in 1933 when Wills defaulted rather than finish the match, "Suddenly there was a dramatic pause! Queen Helen instead of changing courts walked to the stand, steely-faced as ever. 'I default.'" The impact for Jewish young women and girls observing this proved noteworthy. "The important thing was that at last the world of women's tennis had a new conqueror. Her name was Helen Jacobs and she appeared, like a spirit of the nineties—short shorts." Jacobs was characterized by Ford as a genuine heroine, who "was the best in a sport that was thought more entertaining to watch when played by women than men" (Ford 139–41).

Jacobs appeared in two more US championship finals, losing both to Alice Marble, but she continued to influence tennis. She played into the early 1940s, wrote numerous books and contributed articles to the press. Jacobs was inducted into the International Tennis Hall of Fame in 1962 in recognition of her tennis achievements.

Of course, the presence and importance of American Jewish women in tennis goes well beyond the achievements of Helen Hull Jacobs, as this study has shown. At a time when American women in general confronted discrimination in sports (and the broader society) these Jewish women competed and succeeded for themselves and as representatives for all Americans to admire, Jews and non-Jews alike. The American Jewish women players on court in the 1920s and 1930s left an indelible imprint on sports, in particular, and American society more generally. As Joel pointed out, "The prowess of women athletics has become a thing to be expected. Women of today are performing feats of strength, endurance and skill that rival the achievements of the man" (Joel, "Jewish Sports Notes," August 27, 1926, 5). Undoubtedly American Jewish women tennis players formed a significant part of the American Jewish women's expanded participation in sport in American culture. In doing so, they changed perceptions and belied stereotypes both among their fellow Jews and in all areas of American culture as well. They not only appreciably helped change how Jews were perceived but how women—whether Jewish or not—should be seen as a force of athletic prowess, and thus to be reckoned with in American sporting heritage.

Works Cited

American Hebrew 7 June 1935: 94; 138.

Biron, Phineas J. "Strictly Confidential: Tid-Bits from Everywhere." *Jewish Criterion* 13 May 1932: 24. The Pittsburgh Jewish Newspaper Project, Carnegie Mellon University Libraries, Pittsburgh, Pennsylvania [PJNP].

———. "Strictly Confidential: : Tid-Bits from Everywhere." *Jewish Criterion* 15 Sept 1933: 63. PJNP.

———. "Strictly Confidential: Tid-Bits from Everywhere." *Jewish Criterion* 13 January 1935: 14. PJNP.

Borish, Linda J. "'An Interest in Physical Well-Being Among the Feminine Membership': Sporting Activities for Women at Young Men's and Young Women's Hebrew Associations." *American Jewish History* 87 (March 1999): 61–93.

———. "'Athletic Activities of Various Kinds': Physical Health and Sport Programs for Jewish American Women." *Journal of Sport History* 26 (Summer 1999): 240–70.

———. "Jewish American Women, Jewish Organizations and Sports, 1880–1940." *Sports and the American Jew*. Ed. Steven A. Riess. Syracuse: Syracuse Univ., 1998. 105–31.

———. "Jewish Sportswomen." *Jews and American Popular Culture. Vol. 3, Sports, Leisure, and Lifestyle*. Ed. Paul Buhle. Westport, CT: Praeger, 2007. 71–101.

"Boston Women Win Sears Cup, 5 to 4." *New York Times* 9 June 1929: 52. ProQuest Historical Newspapers: *New York Times (1851–2010)* with Index (1851–1993).

Brylawski, Emma. "Womankind: Jewish Women in Sports." *The Jewish Exponent* 3 May 1935: 5. ProQuest Historical Newspapers: *The Jewish Exponent* (1887–1990).

"Charges Bias." *Observer* 5 Sept. 1935: 8.

Cohen, Haskell. "The Sport Year." *Jewish Criterion* 7 Sept. 1934: 179. PJNP.

Conzel, Harry. "Jews Gain High National Rankings in Tennis." *Jewish Criterion* 11 Jan. 1936: 7. PJNP.

———. "Jews in the Nation's Sports." *Jewish Criterion* 27 Sept. 1935: 98, 161. PJNP.

———. "Our Sporting Column." *Jewish Criterion* 24 April 1925: 44. PJNP.

———. "Parade of Jewish Champions In the World of Sports." *Jewish Criterion* 11 Sept. 1936: 87. PJNP.

Danzig, Allison. "Met Tennis Crow to Miss Greenspan." *New York Times* 16 June 1929: S1. ProQuest Historical Newspapers: *New York Times (1851–2010)* with Index (1851–1993).

———. "Miss Francis Loses to Miss Greenspan." *New York Times* 14 June 1925: 35. ProQuest Historical Newspapers: *New York Times (1851–2010)* with Index (1851–1993).

———. "Miss Hirsh [sic] Loses to Miss Taubele." *New York Times* 14 June 1933: 23. ProQuest Historical Newspapers: *New York Times (1851–2010)* with Index (1851–1993).

———. "Miss Greenspan Wins Ardsley Tennis Final." *New York Times* 24 Sept 1928: 17. ProQuest Historical Newspapers: *New York Times (1851–2010)* with Index (1851–1993).

———. "Miss Wills Retains National Net Crown." *New York Times* 28 Aug. 1928: 26. ProQuest Historical Newspapers: *New York Times (1851-2010)* with Index (1851-1993).

———. "Net Fame Sought By Another Helen: Miss Jacobs Arrives Here From Coast and Starts Practice Matches." *New York Times* 9 July 1927: 10. ProQuest Historical Newspapers: *New York Times (1851-2010)* with Index (1851-1993).

Engelmann, Larry. *The Goddess and the American Girl: The Story of Suzanna Lenglen and Helen Wills*. New York: Oxford Univ., 1988.

Ford, Mary Elizabeth. *Little Women Grow Bold*. Boston: Humphries, 1936.

Gallico, Paul. *The Golden People*. Garden City, NY: Doubleday, 1965.

Gems, Gerald R., Linda J. Borish, and Gertrud Pfister. *Sports in American History: From Colonization to Globalization*. Champaign, IL: Human Kinetics, 2008.

Gillmeister, Heiner. *Tennis: A Cultural History*. New York: New York Univ., 1998.

Gould, Alan J. "Mrs. Moody Defaults: Helen Jacobs Triumphs." *Los Angeles Times* 27 Aug. 1933: 1; Pt. 4, 1. ProQuest Historical Newspapers: *Los Angeles Times* (1881-1990).

Gumpert, Bertram Jay. "A Rising Star, Clara Greenspan, Winner of Many Championships." *American Hebrew* 123 (3 Aug. 1928): 389.

"Helen Jacobs Leads Women Athletic Stars. *Atlanta Constitution* 10 Dec. 1933: 10. ProQuest Historical Newspapers: *Atlanta Constitution* (1868-1945).

"Helen Jacobs Makes Debut in 'Scanties': National Tennis Champion Dons Shorts Today for First Time in Public Appearance." *Los Angeles Times* 15 Aug. 1933: A9. ProQuest Historical Newspapers: *Los Angeles Times* (1881-1990).

"Helen Jacobs Tops Nation's Athletic Poll: Net Queen Voted Best in Land." *Los Angeles Times* 20 Dec. 1933: 10. ProQuest Historical Newspapers: *Los Angeles Times* (1881-1990).

"Helen Jacobs Wins English Tennis Crown: Achieves Her Goal After 8 Years of Trying." *Chicago Daily Tribune* 5 July 1936: A9. ProQuest Historical Newspapers: *Chicago Tribune* (1849-1990).

"Honor Roll of Jews in Sports—5696." *American Jewish Outlook* 18 Sept 1936: 20. PJNP.

"Honors Helen Jacobs." *The Review* 18 (17 Feb 1936): 2. Box 2, Periodicals and Publications, Folder, *The Review*. Young Men's and Young Women's Hebrew Association of Philadelphia records undated, 1875-1975, I-241. American Jewish Historical Society, New York, NY and Newton Centre, MA.

Jacobs, Helen Hull. *Beyond the Game: An Autobiography*. Philadelphia: Lippincott, 1936.

———. *Gallery of Champions*. New York: Barnes, 1949.

"Jews Gain High National Rankings in Tennis." *Jewish Criterion* 17 Jan. 1936: 7. PJNP.

Joel, George. "Clara Greenspan Wins her First 1929 Title." *The Sentinel* 94.13 (28 June 1929): 13. The Asher Library, The Spertus Institute for Jewish Learning and Leadership, Chicago, IL. Online Resources, *The Sentinel* (1911-1949).

———. "Jewish Sports Notes." *Jewish Criterion* 16 July 1926: 31. PJNP.

———. "Jewish Sports Notes." *Jewish Criterion* 27 Aug. 1926: 5. PJNP.

———. "Jewish Sports Notes." *Jewish Criterion* 28 Jan. 1927: 15. PJNP.

———. "Jewish Sports Notes." *The Sentinel* 94.10 (7 June 1929): 18. The Asher Library, The Spertus Institute for Jewish Learning and Leadership, Chicago, IL. Online Resources, *The Sentinel* (1911–1949).

———. "Jewish Sports Notes," *The Sentinel* 94.11 (14 June 1929): 13. The Asher Library, The Spertus Institute for Jewish Learning and Leadership, Chicago, IL. Online Resources, *The Sentinel* (1911–1949).

———. "Jewish Sports Notes." *Jewish Criterion* 22 June 1928: 23. PJNP.

———. "Jewish Sports Notes." *Jewish Criterion* 29 June 1928: 27. PJNP.

———. "Jewish Sports Notes." *Jewish Criterion* 20 July 1928: 27. PJNP.

———. "Jewish Sports Notes." *Jewish Criterion* 7 Sept. 1928: 16A. PJNP.

———. "Jewish Sports Notes." *Jewish Criterion* 5 Oct. 1928: 40. PJNP.

———. "Jewish Sports Notes." *Jewish Criterion.* 21 June 1929: 44. PJNP.

———. "The Year in Sports." *Jewish Criterion* 2 Sept. 1927: 29. PJNP.

———. "The Year in Sports." *Jewish Criterion.* 19 Sept. 1927: 368. PJNP.

Kupcinet, Irv. "Jewish Champions Hold Spotlight in Almost Every Field of Sport." *Jewish Advocate* 15 Sept. 1936: 25. ProQuest Historical Newspapers. *The Jewish Advocate* (1905–90).

———. "The World of Sport." *The Observer* (Nashville) 7 May 1936: 8.

Levine, Peter. *Ellis Island to Ebbets Field: Sport and the American Jewish Experience.* New York: Oxford Univ., 1992.

———. "'Our Crowd at Play': The Elite Jewish Country Clubs in the 1920s." *Sports and the American Jew.* Ed. Steven A. Riess. Syracuse: Syracuse Univ., 1998. 160–84.

Mann, David. "Chat O' Books: Jewish Literary News and Notes." *Jewish Criterion* 24 July 1936: 15. PJNP.

Messenger, Janet Graveline. "Helen Hull Jacobs." *WomenSports* (April 1977): 14–16.

"Miss Jacobs Is Speedy Afoot: Needs Competition to Develop Into a Great Star." *Washington Post* 11 Nov. 1925: 19. ProQuest Historical Newspapers: *Washington Post* (1877–1997).

"Miss Surber Loses in Tennis Upset: Top Seeded Player Bows to Miss Hirsch, 13, in Junior Girls' Centre Tourney." *New York Times* 29 Aug. 1930: 22. ProQuest Historical Newspapers: *New York Times (1851–2010)* with Index (1851–1993).

"Miss Taubele Wins with Mother's Aid." *New York Times* 10 Sept. 1927.

"'Mrs. Moody Did Right', Declares Helen Jacobs." *Chicago Daily Tribune* 30 Aug. 1933: 25. ProQuest Historical Newspapers: *Chicago Tribune* (1849–1990).

"Net Title to Miss Hirsch." *New York Times* 26 June 1930: 26. ProQuest Historical Newspapers: *New York Times* (1851–2010) with Index (1851–1993).

"Norma Taubele Wins N.Y. Women's Tennis Title." *Observer* 25 June 1936: 8.

Neumark, Martha. "Lights of New York." *Jewish Criterion* 3 Aug. 1934: 28. PJNP.

"Nine Women Tennis Players Are Selected on Eastern L.T.A. Sears Cup Combination." *New York Times* 2 June 1931: 40.

"Notes of Interest." *Jewish Criterion* 5 July 1935: 25. PJNP.

Pegler, Westbrook. "Miss Wills Wins Battle of the Helens; Retains Title." *Chicago Daily Tribune* 28 Aug. 1928: 17. ProQuest Historical Newspapers: *Chicago Tribune* (1849–1990).

"Sport." *Newsweek* 2 Sept. 1933: 18–20.

"Sport." *Time* 28.11 (14 Sept. 1936): cover and 36–45.

Theis, Grover. "Miss Norma Taubele is Tennis Victor." *New York Times* 20 Sept. 1929: 36. ProQuest Historical Newspapers: *New York Times* (1851–2010) with Index (1851–1993).

Tingay, Lance. *Tennis: A Pictorial History*. Forward by Allison Danzig. New York: Putnam, 1973.

"U. S. Women Tennis Stars Plan to Adopt Stockingless Mode in Play at Wimbledon." *New York Times* 23 May 1929: 37. ProQuest Historical Newspapers: *New York Times* (1851–2010) with Index (1851–1993).

Weiner, Morris. "Jewish Athletes Prove Noble Sportsmen in 5699." *American Jewish Outlook* 8 Sept. 1939: 121. PJNP.

———. "Jewish Sports Champions on Parade." *Jewish Advocate* 3 Sept. 1937: 27. ProQuest Historical Newspapers. *The Jewish Advocate* (1905–90).

———. "Sports Outlook." *American Jewish Outlook* 30 July 1937: 16. PJNP.

———. "The Sports World." *American Jewish Outlook* 30 Aug. 1935: 12. PJNP.

———. "Who's Who in Women's Tennis: Helen Jacobs." *Chicago Daily Tribune* 27 Aug. 1935: 18. ProQuest Historical Newspapers: *Chicago Tribune* (1849–1990).

Answering to a Different Authority in Sports: The Trials of Coach Jonathan Halpert and the Limits of Yeshiva University's Athletic Success in Basketball

by Jeffrey S. Gurock

It was a contest that was emblematic of Coach Jonathan Halpert's forty-two years at the helm of Yeshiva University's (YU) men's basketball team. On November 26, 2013, he led his Maccabees onto the court of their home gym in Washington Heights against the Golden Eagles of St. Joseph's College, a middle-level opponent within the New York Metropolitan area's Skyline Conference. In prior years, St. Joe's had ended up near the top of the heap; in fact, two seasons earlier, when they finished first in regular season play, they had beaten Yeshiva handily. Their most decisive victory was a 32-point blowout on the "Macs'" home court (*Skyline Conference*).[1] But the Golden Eagles' last two recruitment classes had not been nearly so successful as in past seasons. Such is the cyclical calculus of success vs. failure for most clubs in NCAA Division III competition, and this gave the Macs some real reason to be hopeful. Indeed, at first glance, the all-Jewish team, made up mostly of secondary day-school youngsters, matched up physically pretty well against a squad of former public and Christian parochial school players, who hailed predominantly from the vicinity of Patchogue, Long Island. In fact, Yeshiva boasted of having the biggest man on the court—a six-foot, six-inch center—and, not surprisingly, YU controlled the opening jump-ball. But during the first ten minutes of the game, the Macs fell behind by as many as ten points, as the visitors drove hard to the hoop and supplemented this inside game with a barrage of three-pointers. Meanwhile, Yeshiva muffed too many makeable shots. However, as the first half drew to a close, Halpert's well-structured motion-offense began to click, particularly his "back-door" patterns which capitalized on the over-aggressiveness of St. Joe's athletes, who looked to steal the ball and rush down court for an easy lay-up or spectacular dunk. By halftime, the gap had been pared down to just two points. A large crowd of home team supporters—it was "Mac Madness" give-away night—cheered on their schoolmates vigorously.

During the second half, it became progressively clear that St. Joseph's quintet had no answer for Halpert's charges and their "moving without the ball" strategy—another way of characterizing plays that left confused defenders leaning the wrong way while Yeshiva's men faked and then slid toward the basket. For those in the know, the Macs were playing old-style New York City basketball; a style unfamiliar to their opponents who prefer to run and shoot. Most noticeably, Halpert's star player scored repeatedly with uncontested lay-up shots, thus showing that he had internalized well his mentor's fundamental teachings. In the meantime the six-foot, three-inch small forward capitalized on St. Joe's confusion by "stepping out" and making his own three-point shots once his defender became preoccupied with trying to block the "back-door." Yeshiva's number-one play-option would net twenty-eight points that evening. Still, the Golden Eagles had their own weapons at hand, and that kept the game close. Throughout the second-half, they unrelentingly pushed the ball towards the basket, relying on their own superior quickness to gain an advantage; often earning free-throws from the "charity" stripe.

Several times, the Yeshiva starting center and his equally tall replacement blocked initial efforts, only to have St. Joe's salvage the play with second-chance points. And when Yeshiva players were back on their heels, St. Joe's own sharpshooters made their three-pointers count. Throughout the last twenty minutes of regulation play, the contest see-sawed back-and-forth with neither team gaining a decisive edge. As the clock ran down, St. Joe's held on to the ball hoping that the final drive to the bucket would secure victory. But their shot fell short. Players for both squads scrambled for the ball and the second half ended with the contest unresolved.

For YU's fans, the game was a classic case of strength vs. guile, and they hoped that Halpert's system would win out in the end. During the opening minutes of overtime play, Yeshiva's approach seemed to have gained the upper hand as the Macs grabbed a four-point lead. But the Golden Eagles responded, and through a series of field goals and foul shots they pulled ahead by two points with just seconds left to play. A crucial turnover had contributed decisively to St. Joe's ever-so-slight advantage. During his final time out, Halpert drew up a last-ditch play for his attentive young men that looked to get the ball in his star's hand for hopefully a winning three-pointer. Before the game resumed and after watching YU's five set themselves on the court, St. Joe's coach called his own time out to strategize against his opponent's scheme. Despite this, Halpert's plan succeeded in giving his best shooter the chance to vindicate his team and exhilarate the crowd with a victorious effort. But a quick double-team by the Golden Eagles forced an off-balanced attempt that bounced off the side of the rim. YU's star slumped to the floor in momentary despair but soon arose to join Halpert and his teammates in the post-game handshake line. Yeshiva's mentor and players left the gymnasium assured that they had done their best—still, their efforts had proven to be just not quite good enough.

A look at the numbers behind this game suggests why and how the Macs lost. For one thing, YU's bench did not have much in the way of depth of high-caliber subs to call in when the top players needed a break. As a result, Yeshiva's number-one star logged forty-three out of a possible forty-five minutes in the overtime game. His teammates on the starting five played a total some 186 of the 225 minutes (82.5%) on the court. (And it would have been more, but one of the stalwarts fouled out in the closing minutes of regulation time, limiting his appearance to thirty-one minutes.) In contrast, the opposition could rely on its top seven contributors who accumulated together almost all of St. Joe's playing time. But beyond the "fatigue factor," there is also the overall performance of the "supporting cast" to consider. While the big man at center hauled in an impressive twenty rebounds—thirteen off the defensive board—he blocked only one shot and failed on six of his ten shots from the field, near or under the basket, and missed three of his six free throws. And then there was the problem of turnovers. The statistics told a grim tale. While Yeshiva surrendered the ball only twice more than the visitors, when these miscues occurred, St. Joe's quickly cashed in with baskets. Superior athleticism gave them a decisive edge. The Macs rarely were able to capitalize on their steals. The margin of St. Joe's edge was a telling fifteen to two.

Of course, there were bright spots to consider, too. Looking ahead, Halpert and his fans anticipated hopefully that their first-year point-guard would increasingly take on a leadership role. The coach had to have been heartened that this former Jewish high school league star scored seventeen points and relinquished the ball only twice. This was a significant improvement. A week earlier, the guard had scored but eighteen points in his first two games combined, while committing nine turnovers. In the match that followed—a Yeshiva win—he netted nineteen points, but along with this there were also six giveaways. Clearly, for this star of the future, the maturation process was going to take a little more time. Still, it was an encouraging sign that this youngster was becoming increasingly attuned to Halpert's "system." He was becoming aware that he could not always take "the ball to the basket" with impunity against talented athletic defenders the way he had so successfully beaten less skilled, less experienced opponents that he had been able to dominate before entering college ball ("Men's Basketball Loses Exciting Game to St. Joseph's-Long Island").

After the Thanksgiving break, the Macs returned to action at their Max Stern Athletic Center against a far more talented foe, the Panthers of the College at Old Westbury. The home team played courageously and intelligently, but it was unable to overcome the gap in athleticism and quickness that favored the Panthers. Yeshiva lost the encounter 80–64. Early on in the game, their disadvantages became readily apparent. While Yeshiva had to work hard for its baskets, Old Westbury scored quickly and turned every mistake the Macs made into two points at the other end. At halftime, the visitors led by twelve points. During the second half, Yeshiva made strong runs at the lead—even at one point cutting the deficit to six points—only to commit crucial turnovers, which Old Westbury was quick to convert to points. As with the St. Joseph's game, YU's turnover ratio that led to quick baskets showed itself to be of critical importance. The Panthers outscored the Maccabees 18–6 in that crucial statistic. A fundamental coaching axiom was fully evident here: It is obviously important that a mentor inspire his charges to give their all and provide strategy within the context of an appropriate system. But in the end, athletic ability remains the most important component in sports success. Indeed, it is only when two teams are closely matched physically that the elements of motivation and intelligent play-calling become the determining factor ("Men's Basketball Loses to Old Westbury").

This unavoidable coaching reality was likewise in play—but this time in YU's favor— when three days later the Macs easily defeated NYU-Poly, one of the weakest teams in the Skyline Conference. Indeed, over the years, Halpert had mentally marked the "Brooklyn Poly Game" (Brooklyn Poly was the opposition's name until 2008, when it was absorbed by New York University) as a contest where his club did hold a physical advantage over the opposition. Even during his most difficult won-loss seasons, he counted on that match-up as a game that the Macs should win. In four decades of coaching, he had lost to Poly only nine times out of the seventy-two games they had played against the Macs. And beginning with the 1993–94 season, the record was 33–1 against this opponent.[2] For Yeshiva, on this early December night, their mentor's system was not a significant factor in their triumph, even though the Macs easily won by twenty-six points. Most notably in this case, it was they who capitalized on their superior quickness and general athleticism to turn Blue Jay mistakes into Maccabee baskets by a two-to-one margin. And much like the Old Westbury game, the losers attempted at several junctures to cut into the winners' early lead. But every time Poly came close, Yeshiva ran off a series of baskets to deflate their opposition. A 21–4 run in the middle of the second half sealed the triumph for Yeshiva ("Men's Basketball Win over NYU Poly").

These three games played over ten days set a pattern for the rest of the year. Predictably, Yeshiva triumphed both home and away against the two lowest ranked teams, Poly and New York Maritime, even if it rankled Halpert that the second time the teams met his club played listlessly against an undermanned Blue Jays squad that dressed just seven players. Unable to capitalize on a fatigue factor that in this contest was in their favor, the Macs prevailed by a mere three points. The offense was in sync but a porous defense kept the contest competitive longer than should have been the case ("Men's Basketball Uses Balanced Scoring"). Conversely, Halpert's team had no answers for the league's five top teams. But the coach had to have been gratified that the Macs lost on the road by only eight points to Old Westbury, although he was frustrated by a last-second loss at home to third place SUNY-Farmingdale ("Feld Scores 28").

The "system" worked, but a missed final-second lay-up shot doomed Yeshiva's chance at an upset against the favored visiting Rams ("Four Players Score in Double Figures"). Thus, a successful season—defined as reaching the playoffs—hinged upon winning two successive home-and-away games, the first against a traditional rival, the Dolphins of the College of Mount St. Vincent at home and the second an away game against St. Joe's, and, along with that the potential, added bonus of getting even with a team that had previously beaten them. Optimism about a post-season berth had abounded in December when the Macs rallied in the second half in their first meeting against the Dolphins and pulled out a six-point win.

The Macs' two stars sparkled that night with the newcomer guard having a particularly strong game, netting twenty-seven points and making eleven of his fourteen free-throws; many of them in the hotly-contested final minutes ("Men's Basketball Powers Past College of Mount Saint Vincent"). But when the opponent from neighboring Riverdale visited Washington Heights seven weeks later, the Dolphins own late game surge brought them to victory by five points. The compelling statistic in that defeat was the star guard's off-night, as he made only three of his thirteen shots from the field; and neither he nor any of his teammates got to the foul line. The outstanding forward did somewhat better shooting 5–13. One of the problems these two outstanding players faced that night (and in other games) was the "combination" defenses that were arrayed against them. Essentially and effectively, opponents focused their energies on stopping Yeshiva's standouts; sometimes double-teaming them, neglecting the other players, who never proved to be much of a factor in these games.

Interestingly, Yeshiva's best player that evening against the Dolphins was its center who went 7–13 from the field and grabbed twelve rebounds ("Twenty Lead Changes and Eleven Ties"). The big man continued to develop an increasing ability to follow Halpert's strategic patterns. Indeed, on a wintry evening late in February against St. Joseph's, he had another "double-double" (seventeen points and ten rebounds), complementing the mercurial guard who that night scored a game-high twenty-one points. However, Yeshiva failed in its mission to Patchogue, as the Golden Eagles came back from a first half three-point deficit to prevail by ten points ("Men's Basketball Led at Halftime"). As a result, the Macs finished behind these two middle-level opponents and were eliminated from a playoff appearance.

Though the 2013–14 season ended on a disappointing note with an overall record of 7–18 (5–13 in conference play) what transpired that year on the court was highly representative and acutely reminiscent of the ups-and-downs of Halpert's entire four-decade coaching career that ended in March 2014. Though he was understandably proud of his 416 victories (although, admittedly these stood against 552 losses) and of a fifteen-year span (1987–2002), where his club finished .500 or above annually, only occasionally did his Macs triumph against the highest rated conference teams or more powerful out-of-conference opponents, even if they often frustrated the eventual victors. On the other hand, when Halpert's well-structured tactical approach was run properly, his charges rarely lost against teams of comparable or lesser athletic ability. Thus, on balance, his teams made the playoffs eleven times in the fourteen years that the Macs played in the Skyline Conference. Even more impressively, four times in his career, Halpert's system helped Yeshiva cobble together enough wins to earn a first–round spot in a regional Eastern College Athletic Conference (ECAC) post-season tournament. Still, even in the best of years, victories were rarely achieved with ease. Remarkably, in less than 45% of their triumphs, did Yeshiva win by more than ten points. Rarely was the coach able to sit quietly on the bench with legs and arms folded, calmly watching the game-clock run down. And through all the years, the Macs never won an in-season or post-season tournament or a conference championship (*Jonathan Halpert*). Perhaps the closest Yeshiva came to reaching that apogee of its competitive success was in 2000. Then the Macs—with a 16-6 regular season record—were seeded second in the Skyline Conference post-season tournament. It was their highest league-ranking ever. But they lost a home game to Mount St. Vincent, whom they had defeated twice in regular league play. Seemingly, Yeshiva, with prospects of securing an NCAA bid, had difficulty being touted as a favorite, especially when one of its star players was hampered by an injury, as was the case that year. After a last second shot by the Dolphins gave them a 53–52 victory, a stunned Coach Halpert sat for a moment on the bench with his head in his hands before rising to congratulate the winning team, after which he walked off to console his demoralized athletes.[3]

Yeshiva University Maccabees, 2013–14 Season. Courtesy Yeshiva University.

A decade later, Halpert sat down with a local newspaper reporter and waxed philosophical about the difficulties and joys of his efforts at Yeshiva. Projecting himself as a teacher of values through sports, he contended that "if you really want to learn how to coach, lose" and then explained that "losing forces you to learn how to really teach, how to motivate, organize and prioritize." And yet, in an unguarded moment, it became apparent that there resided within the coach, the frustration of never reaching an athletic pinnacle, as he ruefully admitted, "I want it [a conference championship], badly" (Richardson).

Several interrelated, endemic problems have always conspired in limiting the extent of Yeshiva's athletic success. The program has had to deal with the ever-improving nature of the opposition, the narrowness of its own talent pool and, most notably, the distinctiveness of this Orthodox Jewish school's temporal and academic challenges. Taken together, these constraints have seemingly left Halpert to pursue what might almost seem a quest for a championship that has always been foredoomed to failure. After all, due to the inherent nature of the *kind* of academic institution Yeshiva is, the Macs have had to face up to challenges that their competitors have not had to deal with, and these have always made it more difficult for them to finally get to the top of the standings.

To begin with, among most teams that Yeshiva faces in Division III basketball, it has only taken the recruitment of one or two star players for a club to quickly ascend to championship-level status. Such was the case, for example, with SUNY-Purchase, which joined the Skyline Conference as of the 2007–08 season. In its initial campaign, the Panthers finished last with a 2–16 conference mark (3–22 overall). They did, however, split their two games against Yeshiva. The following year, Purchase was on the rise, as they won ten conference games and ended up in the middle of the pack. Their breakout year took place just a season later in 2009–10, when the Westchester-based club won the Conference post-season championship and garnered an invitation to the Division III NCAA tournament. The following year, the Panthers won it all, as they captured both the regular season title with a 17–3 mark (24–5 overall) and the post-season tournament. Once again they capped off their season with an invitation to the NCAA tournament (*Skyline Conference*). Interestingly, during that first championship run, Yeshiva twice upset Purchase by six- and then two-point margins. This achievement earned Halpert "Coach of the Year" league-honors. It was publicly noted that "Halpert who completed his 38th season as the Maccabees' head coach had always gotten the most out of his players and this season was no different." However, during tournament time, Yeshiva succumbed to the Panthers by fifteen points and their opponents emerged as the Skyline Tournament champion to become an NCAA qualifier. In the four years that followed, Yeshiva dropped every Purchase game by an average of over fifteen points as SUNY-Purchase became a dominant power in the league ("Skyline Men's Basketball All-Conference Team Unveiled"; "Skyline Conference Men's Basketball Report 2009–10").

Arguably, the key to the Panthers' rapid rise to success was the unanticipated, but warmly-welcomed, arrival on campus in 2008 of an exceptional player. As a top high school player, Marvin Billups from Chester, New York was widely-recruited by many Division I teams. As Purchase lore has it, this "Gatorade All-American" was ticketed for St. John's University until a serious illness caused the Red Storm to back off from their pursuit of him. A frustrating freshman year at University of New Haven, a strong Division II school, left Billups anxious "to play right away." This was, not surprisingly, a commitment that Panther-coach Jeff Charney was happy to honor. Billups, in turn, demonstrated his own dedication to the program, as he brought with him to Purchase two New Haven teammates, his cousin Corey Orgias and Charles Thompson. With these three stellar scorers in the line-up, success was all but assured. During the two championship years, Billups twice garnered the Skyline Conference's "Player of the Year" designation, and in 2011 he was honored as a Second Team All-American. Perhaps, more important for his school, Billups and his two teammates began to establish a winning tradition, upon which Coach Charney could then build. After graduation, Billups went on to play professional basketball in Puerto Rico (Ciafardini; "Former Purchase Standout Marvin Billups Shining in Puerto Rico").

Of course, Yeshiva has not been entirely lacking when it comes to its own well-plumbed recruitment streams. But rarely do these personnel sources provide Halpert with the type of elite player who can help the Macs compete on a level with opponents like Panthers-star Billups. Most Yeshiva athletes come to Washington Heights from out of the network of Jewish day-schools across the country, as well as the many Orthodox Jewish schools in the NYC metropolitan area. These are rarely the places to find athletic stars.

Annually, the best competitors come to campus on a recruitment trip courtesy of the "National Jewish" Red Sarachek Basketball Tournament. This event is named for Yeshiva's legendary coach—who also served as Halpert's mentor—when he patrolled the sidelines from the 1940s to the early 1970s. This athletic gathering, held since 1992, has brought literally thousands of players to Halpert's attention and thus given him the opportunity to look them over in-person. In its wake, the "Sarachek" has been emulated by any number of regional day-school tournaments, some of which Halpert has attended to scout the best of the yearly crop. Over the years, many of the players who have showed off their abilities at Yeshiva's Sarachek Tournament have returned to New York after high school graduation and a "gap-year" of Torah study in Israel. However, only the most skilled of these standouts within the circumscribed yeshiva sports world have had the ability to match up against the foremost opponents on the college's schedule. While in its twenty-three years of competition, forty-three players from the tournament have played one or more years at Yeshiva, only one ever earned the Most Valuable Player award from the Skyline Conference while two others gained significant recognition as rookies of the year (Yeshiva University 23rd Annual Red Sarachek Basketball Tournament; *Jonathan Halpert*).[4]

Whatever their natural abilities, their success on this next level is undermined by having rarely played as school-boys against top-flight non-Jewish competition. In the case of the Metropolitan area schools situated in and around New York City, Long Island, Westchester New Jersey—where, as of 2014, there were some eighteen clubs in their league—almost the entire schedule pits them against one or another local, fellow day-school athletes. The only exception is when they are invited to out-of-town tournaments, where they do get a chance to face comparably skilled or weaker teams.

These New Yorkers are the best of the local talent. Such athletes and the others with national Jewish day school reputations also stand out when they play on counselor teams at Orthodox-run summer camps in the Catskills or the Poconos. They are the luminaries in the Orthodox versions of the legendary "Five Star" Basketball camp, where the top-flight school boys come from all over the US to upgrade and display their abilities in front of scores of eager Division I coaches (*Metropolitan Yeshiva High School Athletic League; Five Star Basketball*). But New York day-school athletes are not part of this elite warm-weather mix and, much like their narrowly-based winter season, they have no such opportunities that might help them to gain confidence through competition against stronger foes.[5]

In comparison, Orthodox day-school athletes in Dallas, Miami, Chicago or even Los Angeles (which has the nation's second largest Jewish community), not to mention those from Kansas City or Memphis, do not maintain exclusive leagues of their own but instead regularly match themselves up against non-Jewish clubs. Still, although some of these teams have won a lot of games and even some championships in their areas, generally they have defeated small private schools that also draw upon their own limited student bodies. Accordingly, most day-school recruits do not possess the athletic pedigree to stack up well against formidable players of Billups' caliber and the other top-flight conference competitors that YU must face.[6]

It has remained for the exceptional ball player, who has the talent and competitive background and has hailed from outside the day-school "system," to carry forward Halpert's dreams of a championship. Actually, Yeshiva's quest for the so-called "public-school kid" dates back a generation before Halpert assumed the Macs reigns as head coach. In 1949, Marvin Hershkowitz, who as a school-boy was the captain of the De Witt Clinton varsity, which in his junior year captured the New York City Public School basketball championship, presented himself to Sarachek ("Bronx Five Victor at Garden, 49–44"). As Yeshiva lore has it, Hershkowitz initially enrolled at City College of New York (CCNY) a year earlier in 1948 and was a member of its highly-touted freshmen team that its coach Bobby Sand boasted was "the greatest [class] ever to come to the college" ("Lavender Freshmen Heading for New Heights"). Replete with many all-city stars, this club would form the core of CCNY's unparalleled triumphant team that in 1950 captured both the NCAA and National Invitational basketball tournaments and thereby became the toast of the town. Sadly, however, a year later, several of these stars would be implicated in a point-shaving scandal that shook their alma mater and the Big Apple community that loved their Beavers to its core.

Hershkowitz, however, was gone from the St. Nicholas Heights campus during both these glory and then scandal-ridden days at CCNY. The issue with the college's program that triggered his departure was not athletic but religious. As a maturing teenager, he had become increasingly attached to Orthodox Judaism and had come to realize that athletic achievement on a rarified level and fidelity to his faith were incompatible. What would he do about non-kosher training meals and games that took place on the Jewish Sabbath? Yeshiva offered him the chance to continue to compete—although at a lower level of play—and still maintain Orthodox observance. For Sarachek, Hershkowitz's decision to come to YU was a godsend; and given the star forward's growing religious commitments, the school tailored a religious studies program for a young man who did not have a day-school educational background. This conformed well with Yeshiva's academic standards for athletes, since the school has always required that all students take a dual curriculum of general and Jewish studies to earn their graduation credits (Gurock, *The Men* 174–75).

In the years that followed this elite player's arrival, Sarachek was able to recruit additional top-flight Jewish public-school players. The school initially helped the coach along by developing further the curriculum that Hershkowitz followed (he would become an observant Orthodox Jew) into a rudimentary "Jewish Studies Program." With a better brand of athlete on the squad, Yeshiva basketball had its heyday in the mid-1950s. In the 1955–56 campaign, the club went 16–2, and over a four-year period (1953–57) they won fifty-one games against only twenty-seven losses. But while Sarachek basked in his success, some faculty, administrators and a goodly number of students were displeased with the direction the "Program" had taken. For unlike Hershkowitz, who was already committed to Orthodoxy before he arrived on campus, many of those who followed him were not. And in fact, they never did buy into the religious strictures of the yeshiva-world. Critics derisively came to refer to the new curriculum as the "Jewish Sports Program," and the word on Amsterdam Avenue was that "these were guys who would shoot baskets, take the college courses and go home." Simply put, they had a hard time fitting into Yeshiva University's religious culture. By the end of the fifties, the Jewish Studies Program's protocol was, "if you are not already committed, you would not be admitted" (Gurock, *The Men* 176–79; Halpert, 228).

By the time Halpert began coaching at Yeshiva, not only had the welcome-mat been pulled out from under the sneakered feet of potential public-school kids, but the actual number of such athletes was steadily declining. In many communities the sports of choice among Jewish youngsters had become golf, tennis and even swimming—country-club athletic pursuits that had been off-limits to their parents and grandparents (Ringer 114–15, 213–15 [Eds. Note: also see the article by Ari Sclar in this volume.]). With the talent-pool shrinking fast, Halpert made a few concerted efforts to bring in a bumper-crop of elite players in 1977–79, when he organized Yeshiva University's High School Jewish Basketball Tournaments. He brought to campus forty-two stars from around the country, including Dan Schayes who would eventually become a professional in the National Basketball Association (NBA). But only four of these players signed up to play for the Macs, and they were day-school youngsters from Long Island and Atlanta, Georgia who were already planning to come Yeshiva anyway. For these Orthodox athletes, Halpert's offer of the opportunity to play college hoops without having to face the dilemmas of Sabbath play and non-kosher food was highly inviting. Moreover, they already had the educational background to handle the university's rigorous dual program of study. The other ballplayers were fundamentally disinterested in Yeshiva's strictures and obligations. Over the more than thirty years that followed, only two American Jewish public-school players would compete under Halpert (Halpert 236–41).

Over the past 15 years (1999–2014), however, there were two much publicized day-school players who *could* have bolstered Yeshiva's squad but who opted instead to try their hand at big-time college basketball within programs that promised, nonetheless, to respect their religious concerns. In 1999, there was the immensely ballyhooed saga of Tamir Goodman—dubbed by an intrigued media as the "Jewish [Michael] Jordan"—whom the University of Maryland courted for a while. In his initial deliberations with the Terrapins' coaches, this star guard from the Baltimore Talmudic Academy was ostensibly promised that he would not be obliged to play on the Sabbath, would be provided kosher food and might even be able to continue his religious studies through U of M's *Chabad* (the Lubavitcher Hasidim outreach specialists), who offered to step up as potential on-the-road tutors. There was even some talk of moving the dates of the multi-million dollar Atlantic Coast Conference (ACC) tournament away from Saturday to accommodate this Jewish player whom his promoters said was "the *emes*" (in Hebrew, literally, the "truth" or, in other words, the "real deal"). At the apogee of the excitement over this unanticipated development within the Orthodox community, Goodman became a symbol for how tolerant and accommodating America had become towards Jews, in general and Orthodox Judaism, in particular. Seemingly, he would not have to deal with the dilemmas Hershkowitz might have faced half a century earlier. Clearly Goodman did not have to—and clearly he did not want to—play at an Orthodox school to compete as a collegian. Eventually, however, Maryland's coaches backed away from their implicit commitments, as they discerned that Goodman was not quite the star they had initially thought him to be. Ultimately, Goodman played for one year at Towson State University, a Mid-Major Division I school that agreed to schedule around the Sabbath. A year later, Goodman was living in Israel, where he had an undistinguished career on one of Israel's minor league professional teams (Gurock, *Judaism's Encounter*, 160-70; Gurock, "The Crowning of a 'Jewish Jordan' " 161-74).

In 2013, the sports world also took notice of Aaron Liberman, a graduate of Valley Torah High School in California, who was not recruited but walked on to the Big Ten's Northwestern University team. Although standing 6 feet 10 inches, he was not viewed by the coaches as a potential star for the Wildcats. Still, many were intrigued by his desire not only to wear a yarmulke but also *zizith* (the fringe garments worn by observant Jewish men) during games. Orthodox Jews were impressed that the Wildcat coaches accepted him on their squad—although there was no talk in Evanston, Illinois about altering the basketball schedule. Liberman determined, after consultation with a sympathetic rabbi that he would walk to Saturday practices and games since in his view "actually, playing basketball is not breaking any of the 39 laws of the Sabbath. But I'll only be taking cold showers afterward because you can't use hot water." Or for that matter, he would not be using a vehicle to get where he needed to be to practice or play games. Still, others within the Orthodox community did not concur with that halachic (religious legal) decision (Strauss).

Ultimately, Liberman remained more a curiosity than a major contributor to the team. Nonetheless, when he was put into his first game for one minute during a blowout loss against Michigan, the *Jewish Telegraphic Agency* ran a story entitled "Against Michigan, Aaron Liberman's Kippah Makes Hoops History." This report, which was circulated to Jewish newspapers nationwide, also noted that after a home game, in which Liberman did not play, he spoke to the crowd about "what it's like to be an Orthodox Jew playing major college hoops." To add to the spirit of the game, "the school handed out approximately 200 purple yarmulkes with an N printed on them to people who attended" (Soclof). Back at Yeshiva, Coach Halpert's take on Liberman—as had been the case with Goodman—was that these Orthodox youngsters belonged at his school and could have helped his program, even if he was unconvinced that either of them would have been the consummate answer to his recruitment needs ("Nachum Welcomed YU's Coach Jonathan Halpert to JM in the AM").[7]

Rather, since the mid-1980s, Halpert has largely put his faith in recruiting Israeli "public school kids." Much like the big time programs that have looked overseas (including in the Jewish State) for talented athletes, Yeshiva's coach has looked high and wide for the type of skilled, battle-tested and mature player that could bolster his team. Ironically and perhaps fittingly, Marvin Hershkowitz, who migrated with his family to Israel in the 1970s, has been among those who have helped identify ball players who possessed the right combination of personal, religious and athletic qualities to succeed on both the court and in the classroom in Washington Heights.

The best possible candidates have been those who grew up in and did well within Israel's pre-professional club system before fulfilling their three years of active military service. (Yeshiva's admissions protocol has tacitly prohibited recruiting those who might wish to avoid the Israel Defense Force by seeking admission to YU.) As youngsters, Israeli athletes have competed in more challenging settings than have their day-school, Orthodox counterparts state-side. These players typically, however, have not been of Division I pedigree; for if that were the case, a school like the University of Connecticut would have had a better chance to attract them with an athletic scholarship. What the Macs' program could offer was the chance to play college basketball in the United States, while also being educated in a quality American university—sometimes with partial need-based financial aid. Halpert did not demand complete Orthodox religious commitment or conformity from these foreign players; only openness to the Jewish studies curriculum, which was the usual deal-breaker if he ever sought to corral an American public-school recruit. To be sure, the Israelis certainly had a leg up over any conceivable domestic candidate when it came to dealing with Yeshiva's educational demands. For one thing, they had no problem in the Hebrew language courses, which obviously were taught in their native tongue.

Though the recruitment saga and strategy differed in each individual case—and not every foreigner adjusted easily to Orthodox Jewish university life—over a twenty-one year period, twenty-six Israelis, including ten captains and the school's all-time leading scorer (a Hershkowitz protégé) contributed significantly to keeping Yeshiva competitive. What they gave the program, beyond their standout statistics, was a physical and mental toughness, so necessary for Yeshiva to win close games that they inevitably faced. It was often said that a player who just a year or so earlier had faced opponents across the Lebanese border or in the Gaza Strip would hardly blanch at having to make a crucial foul shot in a mere basketball game. When the Israelis' skills were melded adroitly into Halpert's system, supplemented by the one or two outstanding American day-school teammates who had been cherry-picked from "the Sarachek," Yeshiva habitually beat the lower level clubs in their conference and more often than not the team held its own against the middle of the pack in their league. And conversely, perhaps the difficulties that the 2013–14 team experienced, when it was ultimately edged out for that final Skyline playoff spot, may be attributed in significant part to the absence, for the first time in a generation of any foreign-born players. The two star-players and the ever-improving center all came out of the day-school system and the Sarachek tournament. In all events, over the years, with this combination of domestic and foreign born players working together, Yeshiva won enough games to be invited to the aforementioned ECAC post-season tournaments. Still, even in their most victorious years, the best Yeshiva might offer was never sufficient to defeat teams that boasted high quality players, nor were they ever able to secure a conference title and with it a coveted NCAA national tournament bid (Halpert 82–87).[8]

Less noticeable than star opponents, but also very much in play in undermining Yeshiva's championship quest, is, ironically Orthodox Judaism's own revered clock and calendar. This temporal problem stems directly from the very religious distinctiveness of which the school is most proud. For in the end, notwithstanding the Goodman and Liberman unique personal scenarios, Yeshiva really is the only school in America where an observant Orthodox Jew can play college-level basketball without violating or severely challenging his Sabbath scruples. Yeshiva basketball is so different, when compared to other colleges with which it competes, that in February 2014 newspaper sports pundit Phil Mushnick was moved to wryly observe: "Aside from being the longest one-school college coach in NYC history, Halpert holds a record that never will be surpassed: His Yeshiva teams never have lost a Friday night or Saturday afternoon game." But with Friday, and most of Saturday out-of-bounds, the Macs have had to cram their games, not to mention their limited practice time, within the confines of the five remaining weekdays. To their credit, opponents have not objected to playing Sunday games, even if they might prefer to have that day off for rest or additional training. Moreover, the NCAA recognizes Yeshiva's right—as it does under similar circumstances for Bingham Young University, whose majority of students are members of the Church of Latter Day Saints—not to have to play on its Sabbath. Such is the enlightened sports policy of a religiously-tolerant United States today. Still, attempting to win back-to-back games or to triumph four times over a week's period, regardless of the opposition, has always posed a daunting challenge to YU. Often that strain has led to injuries among these overworked and under-practiced athletes (Mushnick; Worthen 128–29).

Mushnick also could have noted an additional scheduling dynamic and dilemma that contributes to an unavoidable fatigue factor. Due to the annual series of September-October Jewish holidays, the school suspends classes for effectively two to three weeks in the middle of the fall semester. Consequently, student-athletes, along with the rest of their schoolmates, finally take their end of semester exams in early to mid-January and then have an intersession break over the remainder of that month. Most other schools take their winter break before and after Christmas in December through the beginning of January. Effectively, this means that Yeshiva has to play what amounts to two half-seasons: December and February (but never on Shabbat, of course), thus leaving them little time for practice and rehabilitation once the season starts up again. To make matters worse during the unsuccessful 2013–14 season, a series of actuarial "acts of God" also interfered with Halpert's schedule, which had been designed and carefully drawn up precisely to mitigate these difficulties as much as this could be done. A series of unanticipated snowstorms during February in the Metropolitan area forced cancellations of what otherwise would have been more properly spaced games. As a result, twice during this period, Yeshiva was forced to play back-to-back games. And during one eight-day period, which extended over two Friday nights and Saturday, the Macs played five games with almost no practice time in-between. They were unsuccessful in every one of these nine engagements (*Yeshiva University Maccabees*. Schedule 2013–14).

Finally, Yeshiva basketball is challenged by the rigor of its academic requirements. No school on its schedule, (except perhaps NYU-"Brooklyn" Poly) requires its student-athletes to attend such a full complement of classes (which can mount up to twenty-nine hours a week) to the extent that is required by this Orthodox academic institution. This reality undermines practice and recovery time in much the same way as the Orthodox calendar does. Even the regularly scheduled practices cannot begin until after 7 pm in deference to the academic program. Over the years, the Macs have played teams on its out-of-conference schedule from some excellent academic institutions and top Division III clubs—NYU, MIT, Brandeis and Emory, for example. But even they do not insist upon the same daunting attendance hours in school as does Yeshiva. Thus in recruitment, Halpert has been stymied by the so called "demands of the dual program"—perhaps as much as the kosher and Sabbath regulations, regardless of whether the candidate is an American or an Israeli.

Still, Coach Halpert is abundantly proud of the recognition his athletes once received from an opposing school that took note of what he and his young men face in attempting to be Orthodox Jewish scholars and athletes. One of his prized mementos from the 1997 ECAC invitation was a sign that was taped to his visitors' locker room door: "Due to class commitment of the Yeshiva student-athletes, our game will tip-off at 8.p.m." Yeshiva lost the game to a more athletic and better-conditioned College of Staten Island team. But in retrospect, the coach would contend that the locker room "announcement remains far more meaningful that any ECAC trophy" (Halpert 30).

Thus, ultimately, for Halpert, the calculus of a once-expressed frustration about his inability to win a championship balanced against his more often reconciled appreciation of Yeshiva basketball realities bespeaks the program's longtime mission ever since a group of students started the team more than eighty years ago. Like the school they have represented, these Orthodox collegians have aspired to live harmoniously within their country's and their faith's cultures, dealing as best they can with the conflicts that inevitably ensue in tentatively embracing a world that is not inherently akin to theirs. As athletes, they pursue the dream of victory—the secular quest for a piece of immortality that comes with raising a trophy high. But, also as committed Jews, they have a higher goal to fulfill the millennia-old vision that their conception of Judaism places before them. For forty-two years, Coach Jonathan Halpert did all that he could to win while still listening to that higher authority (Gurock, "The Beginnings" 157–72).

Notes

1. In the 2011–12 season, St. Joseph's went 17-1 in the regular season, only to be upset in the conference championship game by SUNY-Purchase. Nonetheless, the Golden Eagles were selected for the Division III NCAA tournament. The next year, St. Joseph's record in conference play was 4-14.
2. For year-by-year statistics on Yeshiva's wins and losses to Poly, see *Jonathan Halpert*.
3. As of the end of the 2013-14 season, Yeshiva won during Halpert's tenure, 188 games by more than ten points: twenty-seven times in total. Brooklyn Poly was the Macs' most unfortunate victim. Two other opponents, Bard College and Pratt Institute lost eighteen and fourteen times respectively by more than ten points. When these games—played against, arguably, their weakest traditional opponents—are factored out, Yeshiva otherwise won by ten points or more only thirty percent of the time. On Halpert's feelings about the loss opportunity vs. Mount St. Vincent, it should be noted that more than a decade later, he would note that "it was the most disappointing loss in my forty-one-year career." He would also note the injury that hampered one of his star players. See Halpert 123.
4. Interestingly, not all of the best players from this cohort have opted for Yeshiva as their college. An informal survey of the recipients of the "Most Valuable Player" awards by the tournament assistant director and statistician indicates that only four of the winners enrolled at Yeshiva. See Bandler.
5. There are in existence several kosher basketball camps for observant youngsters that emulate what Five Star does generally. See, for example, *Step It Up*, which boasts that players come from eighteen states and ten foreign countries to be offered its glatt-kosher cuisine, sports and religious studies. But, here again the Orthodox youngsters are playing against one another.
6. Perhaps the best out of (New York) town school over the past few decades has been the Yeshiva University of Los Angeles [YULA]. For example, The 2012 YULA Panthers varsity basketball team went 27-7 overall, winning the Cooper, Milken, Hillcrest Christian and Sarachek Tournaments. See on their recent record, "Sweat Equity."
7. During the years of the Sarachek tournament, three other day school players "walked on" and played sporadically at Division I programs, although with less notoriety. See *Jonathan Halbert*.
8. In addition to the Israelis, who were recruited from overseas in the 1980s on an annual basis, Yeshiva also recruited two brothers, who were originally from Israel but who had moved to the US with their parents, after playing club-basketball back in their original home. They proved to be effective, if unusually acquired "American" public-school players, who found their way to Yeshiva through friends of the school, residing in Atlanta, GA. These two helped lead the school to the ECAC tournament. Finally, an Argentinian recruit, who had played higher-level youth basketball in his own country, likewise aided the program in the early 2010s. See Halpert 76-77, 78-81.

Works Cited

Bandler, Jonathan. Email to Jeffrey S. Gurock. 26 Feb. 2014.

"Bronx Five Victor at Garden, 49–44." *New York Times* 23 Mar. 1947: 53.

"Feld Score 28, Weissberg Has Double-Double but Men's Basketball Falls Short at Old Westbury." *Yeshiva University Maccabees*, 9 Feb. 2014. 14 Aug. 2014 <http://yumacs.com/news/2014/2/9/MBB_0209144312.aspx?path=mbball>.

Ciafardini, Robert. "Back to Back P of Y Billups Tourney MVP Lead Way." *Purchase College: State University of New York*, 12 Mar. 2011. 14 Aug. 2014 <https://www.purchase.edu/departments/PhysicalEducation/mensbasketball/default.aspx>.

———. Personal interview. 3 Feb. 2014.

Five Star Basketball. Camps. 13 Aug. 2014 <http://www.fivestarbasketball.com/camps>.

"Former Purchase Standout Marvin Billups Shining in Puerto Rico." *Skyline Conference*, 17 Nov. 2011. 14 Aug. 2014 <http://www.skylineconference.org/news/2011/11/17/MBB_1117110946.aspx>.

"Four Players Score in Double Figures as Men's Basketball Loses Close One to Farmingdale State." *Yeshiva University Maccabees*, 12 Feb. 2014. 14 Aug. 2014 <http://yumacs.com/news/2014/2/12/MBB_0212143430.aspx?path=mbball>.

Gurock, Jeffrey. "The Beginnings of Team Torah u-Madda: Sports and the Mission of an Americanized Yeshiva, 1916–1940." *The Torah u-Madda Journal* 14 (2006–07): 157–72.

———. "The Crowning of a 'Jewish Jordan': Tamir Goodman, the American Sports Media and Modern Orthodox Jewry's Fantasy World." *Studies in Jewish Civilization: American Judaism in Popular Culture*. Ed. Leonard Jay Greenspoon and Ronald Simkins. Omaha, NE: Creighton Univ., 2007. 161–74.

———. *Judaism's Encounter with American Sports*. Bloomington: Indiana Univ., 2005.

———. *The Men and Women of Yeshiva: Orthodoxy, Higher Education and American Judaism*. New York: Columbia Univ., 1988.

Halpert, Jonathan. *Are You Still Coaching? 41 Years Coaching Yeshiva University Basketball*. Bloomington: Authorhouse, 2013.

Jonathan Halpert: The Official Website of Head Coach Dr. Jonathan Halpert. 2014. 13 Aug. 2014 <http://www.jonathanhalpert.com>.

"Lavender Freshmen Heading for New Heights." *The Campus: The Undergraduate Newspaper of the City College* 30 Sept. 1948: 7.

"Men's Basketball Earns Big Skyline Win over NYU Poly." *Yeshiva University Maccabees*, 4 Dec. 2013. 14 Aug. 2014 <http://yumacs.com/news/2013/12/4/MBB_1204134259.aspx>.

"Men's Basketball Led at Halftime, But Fell to St. Joseph's-Long Island." *Yeshiva University Maccabees*, 18 Feb. 2014. 14 Aug. 2014 <http://yumacs.com/news/2014/2/18/MBB_0218142701.aspx>.

"Men's Basketball Loses Exciting Game to St. Joseph's-Long Island." *Yeshiva University Maccabees*, 26 Nov. 2013. 14 Aug. 2014 <http://yumacs.com/news/2013/11/26/MBB_1126132638.aspx?path=mbball>.

"Men's Basketball Loses to Old Westbury." *Yeshiva University Maccabees*, 2 Dec. 2013. *14 Aug. 2014* <http://yumacs.com/news/2013/12/2/MBB_1202133311.aspx?path= mbball>.

"Men's Basketball Powers Past College of Mount Saint Vincent." *Yeshiva University Maccabees*, 13 Dec. 2013. 14 Aug. 2014 <http://yumacs.com/news/2013/12/13/MBB_1213131850.aspx?path=mbball>

"Men's Basketball Uses Balanced Scoring and Great Ball Distribution in Win over NYU Poly." *Yeshiva University Maccabees*, 27 Jan. 2014. 14 Aug. 2014 <http://yumacs.com/news/2014/1/27/MBB_0127144858.aspx?path=mbball>.

Mushnick, Phil. "The Book on Yeshiva Coach." *The New York Post*, 8 Feb. 2014. 14 Aug. 2014 <http://nypost.com/2014/02/08/tv-deals-tend-to-dictate-networks-olympic-slant/>.

Metropolitan Yeshiva High School Athletic League. Schedule. 13 Aug. 2014 <http://www.myhsal.com/schedule/>.

"Nachum Welcomed YU's Coach Jonathan Halpert to JM in the AM to Explore his Book 'Are You Still Coaching.'" *JM in the AM radio archive WFMU Radio*. 14 Jan. 2014. Radio.

Richardson, Clem. "Longtime Maccabees Coach Jonathan Halpert Has His Own Philosophy on Winning." *Daily News*, 12 Mar. 2012. 14 Aug. 2014 <http://www.nydailynews.com/new-york/longtime-maccabees-coach-jonathan-halpert-philosophy-winning-article-1.177007>.

Ringer, Benjamin R. The *Edge of Friendliness: A Study of Jewish-Gentile Relations*. New York: Basic, 1967.

Skyline Conference. Archives. 13 Aug. 2014 <http://www.skylineconference.org/archives.aspx?path=>.

"Skyline Men's Basketball All-Conference Team Unveiled." *Skyline Conference*, 2 Mar. 2001. 13 Aug. 2014 <http://www.skylineconference.org/news/2011/3/2/MBB_0302115838.aspx>.

"Skyline Conference Men's Basketball Report 2009-10 All-Skyline Conference." *Skyline Conference*. 14 Aug. 2014 <http://www.skylineconference.org/documents/2010/3/2/2010_all_skyline_mbb.pdf?id=945>.

Soclof, Adam. "Against Michigan, Aaron Lieberman's Kippah Makes Hoops History." *Canadian Jewish News*, 7 Jan. 2014. 14 Aug. 2014 <http://www.cjnews.com/sports/against-michigan-aaron-liberman%E2%80%99s-kippah-makes-hoops-history>.

Step It Up Basketball. 13 Aug. 2014 <http://www.timetostepitup.com>.

Strauss, Ben. "Studying X's and O's and the Torah." *New York Times,* 27 Jan. 2013. 14 Aug. 2014 <http://www.nytimes.com/2013/01/28/sports/ncaabasketball/northwesterns-aaron-liberman-studies-xs-os-and-torah.html?pagewanted=all&_r=0>.

"Sweat Equity: Taking Sarachek Championship is a Happy Ending for Varsity Seniors." *Yeshiva University of Los Angeles: Boys High School*, 30 Mar. 2012. 14 Aug. 2014 <http://www.yulaboys.org/apps/news/show_news.jsp?REC_ID=245504&id=0>.

"Twenty Lead Changes and Eleven Ties in Men's Basketball Game against Mt. St. Vincent." *Yeshiva University Maccabees*, 4 Feb. 2014. 14 Aug. 2014 <http://www.yumacs.com/news/2014/2/4/MBB_0204142749.aspx?path=mbball>.

Worthen, Kevin J. "The NCAA and Religion: Insights About Non-State Governance from Sunday Play and End Zone Celebrations." *Utah Law Review* 2010 (2010): 123–40.

Yeshiva University 23rd Annual Red Sarachek Basketball Tournament, March 27–31, 2014. New York: Yeshiva Univ., 2014. Unpublished program.

Yeshiva University Maccabees. Schedule 2013–14. 14 Aug. 2014 <http://yumacs.com/schedule.aspx?schedule=98&path=mbball>.

"The Disadvantage Far Outweighs the Benefits": How the Rise and Fall of "the Jewish Game" at the 92nd Street YMHA Exemplified Jewish Conceptions of Athleticism

by Ari F. Sclar

In 1891, in the midst of America's transformation into an urban, industrial society, basketball was invented at the YMCA (Young Men's Christian Association) as a way to teach the "right kind of manhood" through clean, amateur play.[1] In the ensuing decades, as Jews found their own space within American sports, Young Men's Hebrew Associations (YMHAs) and Jewish Community Centers (JCCs) hoped in a similar fashion to use sports to serve the dual purpose of Americanizing the children of immigrants and dispelling stereotypes of Jewish physical weakness and inferiority (Levine, *Ellis Island to Ebbets Field*; Riess). Jewish institutional basketball paralleled the rise of a Jewish basketball culture that peaked during the interwar period and then rapidly declined in the post-World War II era. But at the height of its popularity, basketball came to be viewed by many as the "Jewish Game," due to the large number of Jewish players in public schools, colleges, and professional leagues.[2] Institutions, such as the 92nd Street YMHA, in particular, used basketball to promote themselves as well as to finance their athletic departments, especially prior to World War II. The standard and somewhat simplistic explanation for the decline of Jewish basketball after the War is that Jews no longer needed to produce top athletes, because they had already successfully integrated into mainstream society. This explanation helps explain the rise and fall of institutional Jewish basketball, at least in part, but it does not take into account the complex, cultural dynamics that shaped the arc of Jewish basketball from success to its decline.

A close look at the unpublished files of the YMHA and other related archives indicates that the actual circumstance was more nuanced and, in fact, reveals a good deal about how Jews thought (and continue to think) about their role, both on the court and off. Rather than existing solely as a positive force, basketball at the 92nd Street YMHA and elsewhere came to be viewed as a mixed bag. Jews at the YMHA had an idealistic concept of what sports—in particular basketball—*should be*, and this had to be weighed against the competitive and commercial pressures inherent to what a sport like basketball *really was*. The inability of the directors of the YMHA and its related institutions to resolve the basic dilemma of their dual-vision of basketball would be partly responsible for the downfall of the institutional culture. And as a result, basketball, which had been the quintessential sport at the YMHAs and JCCs, was the "Jewish Game" no longer.

Founded in 1874, the New York YMHA (renamed the 92nd Street YMHA in 1900) developed an extensive program of literary, social, educational, and religious classes and clubs in its early years. Physical activity, however, remained only a minimal part of the broader program, and in May 1890, YMHA director H. Pereira Mendes addressed "our failure to provide attraction for our young men." The YMHA could not compete with organizations such as the "German Halle near our institution," which offered "gymnastic instruction and that active exercise in which all healthy men take delight." Mendes believed that sports and recreation needed to become a more prominent component of the Association and would function as a means to attract Jewish young men (Mendes, Letter to the President and Directors of the YMHA, May 24, 1890). The YMHA briefly established a Committee on Physical Culture and offered billiards, checkers, and chess to its membership. In 1897, officials suggested "forming of a baseball or bicycle club for the summer to attract the Jewish young men of the neighborhood" (Board of Directors, YMHA, "Minutes," June 1893–January 1898). Some "young men," who wanted a more formal athletic environment, formed the YMHA Athletic Club in 1898 as a member-controlled but subordinate organization within the larger YMHA. Within weeks of the club's founding, however, the YMHA's superintendent suspended a prominent member "for boisterous conduct in the Gym," and for "refusing to stop his tomfoolery" ("William Mitchell Journal," September 21, 1898). Despite this incident, Association officials recognized the club's importance since it "promotes good-fellowship among the Gymnasium members and helps maintain the grade of work."[3] Nonetheless, Mendes' plea did not directly lead to the development of competitive sports in the 1890s, as the athletic club focused exclusively on gymnastics, and there was no mention of basketball at the Association during the decade. This may have been due in part to the limitation of the facilities, and the YMHA eventually did expand beyond the general gymnasium work of calisthenics and gymnastic exhibitions after the construction of a new building on 92nd Street in May 1900. Interestingly, at least to judge from the data in the YMHA's own files, the emergence of the stereotype of the weak unathletic Jew during the 1890s seemingly had little initial impact on the institutional thinking in developing the athletic program.

Still, outside the Association's walls, this was very much a live issue. Sports' widening popularity in the late nineteenth century led to comparisons of the athletic abilities of different nations, and some commentators noted Jews' absence from the annals of sports history. In 1892, George Alfred Townsend argued in *The Chatauquan*: "the law of Moses, omitting social and athletic amusements ... weakened his [the "Hebrew's"] moral influence while making him commercially eminent and superior." Three years later, the *North American Review* celebrated Anglo-Saxon physical superiority in comparison to other "civilized nations" and charged: "The Jews, who alone refuse active exertion, either as a means of livelihood or as a source of amusement, are perhaps the sole instance of a successful people ... who explicitly or implicitly reject the duty of exercise; this no doubt is a survival of the oriental feeling that the burden of labor should fall on slaves." Similar in tone, though with less derogatory rhetoric, the elite sporting magazine *Outing* noted in 1899 that, "the Jews in all nations and times have produced ... their share of leaders in art, in drama, in music, in literature, and in law; in fact, in all those walks of life in which intellectual acumen and close application to books, and to the study of mankind, is the main force; but they have hitherto, as a people, shown little aptitude for, or application to, the sports of the field and of sustained interest in outdoor recreation" (Jones 639–40; Turner 452).

In these articles, one can see the depiction of "the Jews" as a group of "90-pound weaklings" (to borrow a term made popular by body-builder Charles Atlas) who had developed intellectual and commercial abilities that compensated for their lack of physical ability. *Outing*'s isolation of Jewish "intellectual acumen" conceded a certain element of praise, but also left the unmistakable implication that traditional Jewish culture simply did not include a physical component. *Outing* praised members of an elite Jewish country club who had "somewhat broken away from tradition" due to the "more settled conditions resulting from their civic and religious freedom in America."[4] The author also indicated that American freedom allowed Jews to overcome perceived negative cultural components that had opposed "outdoor recreation." These articles brought no response from Association officials, and there was minimal attention given to the stereotype in the *Bulletin* in the early 1900s. It is unclear whether such rhetorical condemnation of Jewish athletic inferiority directly impacted and influenced the leadership policy of the YMHA, but what is clear is that basketball initially served an institutional purpose that had little to do with the stereotype of the weak Jew.

Institutional basketball is often portrayed as being used by the leadership as a way to dispel stereotypes, but at the YMHA it was the members rather than officials who initiated the formation of a basketball team.[5] The initial notice of YMHA basketball occurred in the November 1900 issue of the institution's *YMHA Bulletin*, and simply noted, "a basket-ball team is being formed." The following month, the *Bulletin* expanded its coverage and declared that the squad "appeared in their new uniforms, and the effect was dazzling." The *Bulletin* also noted that a series of victories was "the best evidence of the pluck and grit of our players" (*YMHA Bulletin*, December 1900). Yet, "pluck and grit" were not necessarily the attributes that YMHA officials wanted its members to learn through basketball. They had a more idealistic vision of what role basketball should play in the development of Jewish manhood. In January 1901, for example, the *Bulletin* again featured the basketball team and stated:

> Our men are beginning to realize the great possibilities for physical improvement to be derived from the game and are doing all in their power to make it clean, healthful, and sportsmanlike. The captain, George Hyman deserves the credit for his endeavors to eliminate all rough playing and make the sport one in which players can win a victory with becoming modesty or accept a defeat without bitter feeling. It rests with the players to make the game all that it should be, and they can then depend upon the good will and active co-operation of the officials of the YMHA. (*YMHA Bulletin*, January 1901)

This passage illustrates a number of issues central to basketball's early development at the 92nd Street YMHA. The importance of keeping the game clean and without "rough playing" was essential to the belief that basketball should impart correct values and behavior when played according to its original intentions. As an instructional game, basketball was intended to teach self-control and cooperative team play, while competitiveness was simply a means to accomplish these ends and not an end unto itself. The clean play of amateur basketball ensured that the game would remain free from the taint of professionalism, which physical educators believed inevitably led to detrimental behaviors such as gambling, disrespect toward officials and opponents, and—the most destructive force of all—victory for its own sake (Horger 40–45). While the *Bulletin* did not explicitly link rough play with professionalism, the passage insinuates that YMHA officials were watching closely and ready to intervene to discourage what they deemed to be improper behavior. When problems arose at the end of 1901, the YMHA quickly moved to eliminate basketball games with outside teams, and while it is unclear whether rough play caused this abandonment, the 1902 *Annual Report* declared that "intense rivalry and limited quarters" influenced the decision.[6] This suspension lasted almost two years, but the attempt to tightly control basketball at the institution proved to be more difficult and required more than the temporary elimination of games against outside teams.

In January 1902, the same month the YMHA suspended competitive basketball, the Association clearly stated its attitude toward sports in a *Bulletin* article entitled "Athletic 'Specialists.'" The article declared that members would "derive great benefit" from physical activities, and warned, "the gymnasium was not to be used for training athletes, but rather for developing the physical condition of its members" (*YMIHA Bulletin*, January 1902). Such an attitude meant that YMHA officials initially desired to keep their distance from the competitive basketball world. Nonetheless, in November 1903, the resumption of outside competition was accompanied by an admission-charge to all games. Unlike the initial admission fee established in 1901, whose aim had been to *decrease* attendance, the new admission charge served purely financial ends and thus was a tacit nod to the commercial advantage that could be offered by basketball for the benefit of the YMHA. Officials requested that "since the money is to go toward the vacation camp fund everybody ought to patronize them [basketball games]" (Sperling).

The same month that the YMHA resumed outside games, it joined the Amateur Athletic Union (AAU), which had taken over as amateur basketball's ruling body after the YMCA stopped trying to control the sport.[7] Basketball was originally viewed by physical educators as an instructional game to shape behavior toward a positive social end by teaching its participants team work, obedience, and what was ambiguously defined as "American" values. Before the end of the 1890s, however, professionalism, commercialism, and rough play intruded on the game's supposed purity and decentralized the sport (Horger 1–35). The AAU realistically understood it could not eliminate professional basketball, but the Union sought to contain it and prevent it from spreading into amateur competition by banning non-registered players and teams from all AAU competitions. In the 1890s, the AAU Basketball Committee had implemented a registration plan to combat the influence of professionalism in basketball and forbade AAU teams from playing even independent, or non-AAU, amateur teams (Horger 67–72).

For the 92nd Street YMHA, membership in the AAU made competitive basketball more visible but, in doing so, it also introduced new pressures that necessitated some practical measures. More serious competition led to organized practice, representative teams, and a hierarchical athletic structure. After the YMHA's representative team went winless in five games at the 1904 Metropolitan AAU championship, the Association hosted the tournament in 1905. The tournament "attracted several thousands [spectators] . . . many of whom had never heard of the Association," and generated almost $150 from tournament receipts for the YMHA. Despite this financial benefit, Association officials maintained the idealistic stance that the AAU tournament was held because of the "belief that all amateur sport should be put on a high plane and kept free from professionalism" ("The Recent Basketball Tournament"; Young Men's Hebrew Association, *Thirty-First Annual Report, 1905*). These same officials also claimed that the AAU tournament directly increased basketball's popularity at the YMHA, as reflected by the presence of more than twenty teams by 1906.

Association officials recognized the sport's popularity and appeal to spectators, but they continued to try to restrain competitive basketball. A 1906 *Bulletin* article entitled "Basketball and Morals" stated:

> A boy who learns by his athletic life to do everything he can honorably to win, but to submit cheerfully to defeat rather than indulge in trickery and meanness, will carry the same spirit in all his recreation, in all his after life . . . it is not simply a question of physical exercise and physical development, but that a great moral question is involved . . . character must be put above victory. Basketball is a splendid game for the making of character one of the best [sic]. ("Basketball and Morals")

Attempts to minimize the importance of athletic specialization conflicted with some members' aspirations, especially those who formed the Atlas Athletic Club, which had changed its name from the YMHA Athletic Club in order to function "without being interfered with by the YMHA." The club had been formed ostensibly to encourage physical culture, but members primarily focused on competitive sports in the early 1900s. They found the YMHA generally unwilling to cater to their desires, and when the club was refused the use of the gymnasium for basketball practice in November 1906, Atlas president Henry Lang informed YMHA officials that the club had decided "to sever its connection . . . it was a case of existing without advancing . . . we have been fully cognizant . . . of the inability of the Association to specialize in the direction of and cater to athletics." At the formal opening of Atlas' new clubhouse, YMHA superintendent William Mitchell told the club, "it is necessary that you stick to your resolution to do purely athletic work, to the end that you may draw to your club the many young Jewish athletes who at present are barred from other clubs" (*YMHA Bulletin,* May 1907). This speech has been viewed as illustrative of Jewish institutional support for sports' inclusion in American Jewish life (Levine, *Ellis Island to Ebbets Field* 15). A closer reading indicates, however, that Mitchell's advocacy for Atlas to "do purely athletic work" may have meant to separate and demarcate its function from that of the YMHA. While the Association would continue to provide a space for general physical exercise, focused on individual development and character, the serious emphasis on sports would be left to Atlas, thus ensuring no conflict between the organizations. Within the year, however, the YMHA's overall attitude changed and resulted in a more complex situation that began to upset the uneasy balance between the idealistic concept of "clean" athletics over against the more pragmatic concern for "specialization."

The trigger for this occurred in December 1907, when Harvard president Charles Eliot, speaking in front of the school's Menorah Society, was quoted in the *New York Times* as having told the audience: "If you take any representative gathering of, say a thousand Jews, you will find that they are distinctly inferior in stature and physical development to a similar gathering of representatives of any other race." President Eliot did not claim that Jews could not physically regenerate, but similar to the article in *Outing* the previous decade, he placed the onus on Jews to change. He believed that the freedom offered by America provided an opportunity for modern Jews to recapture the "glorious times in the history of the Jews when there was a martial spirit among you." Eliot indicated that Jewish physical inferiority occurred because of centuries of suffering, but also claimed: "Here at Harvard, you young men, members of the Jewish race, neglect the out-of-door life, and do not get out into the fresh air and develop physically as you should, although you are taking every advantage of the intellectual opportunities offered you" ("Urges Jews to be Strong").

Eliot's comments, which simplistically assumed a unified Jewish cultural and racial identity that included both physical deficiency and lack of physical activity, received an immediate, public, and anxious response from American Jews. During an era when the immigration restriction movement gained strength, and many Americans believed that immigrants could not, or would not, assimilate, Jewish newspapers in Denver, St. Louis, Detroit, Pittsburgh, and elsewhere published editorials, letters, and rabbinical sermons on the subject of the supposed physical weakness of Jews. Most commentary focused on Eliot's condemnation of Jewish anemic physicality. Some Jews posited "vitality" as an alternative definition of physicality in order to illustrate that traditional Judaism promoted health. Rabbi Joseph Silverman of New York's prestigious Temple Emanu-El denied that Jews, including eastern European Jewish immigrants, had ever degenerated, and claimed "stature and development are matters of leisure." Rabbi Samuel Margolies of Cleveland's Anshe Emeth agreed and stated that, "the best authorities on this subject . . . call attention to the pronounced vitality of the Jews and to their physical strength" ("Rabbi Excerpts to Eliot Speech"; Editorial, *Jewish Outlook*; also see "Rabbi Chas. Fleischer's Reply to President Eliot"; "President Eliot at the Menorah Society"; Editorial, *Jewish Criterion*).

Eliot's comments also received attention at the 92nd Street YMHA, where a *Bulletin* editorial agreed that, "our Jewish young men are not sufficiently developed physically," and claimed that the relatively limited number of Jewish athletes served as "the best proof of this." The solution would be for "the Jewish philanthropist to remove the stigma by giving larger support than heretofore to institutions like the YMHA," which was "engaged in the all-around development of young men" ("Are the Jews Really Inferior?"). Perhaps it was not entirely coincidental that officials extended the YMHA's commitment to competitive sports in the 1908 annual report. "We hope some day to see some of our own boys take a prominent part in athletic competition and thus disprove that our people do not give proper attention to our physical development" (Young Men's Hebrew Association, *Thirty-Fourth Annual Report, 1908*). Finally, in October 1908, a *Bulletin* editorial stated: "Let us therefore from now on determine to win honors in the athletic world . . . the Association will do its share toward encouraging athletics in the building" ("Athletics in the YMHA").

Officials blamed the lack of athletes on the absence of communal support for institutions interested in "all-around development." The YMHA hoped to show that it offered programs unavailable elsewhere in organized Jewish communal life and thus deserved more attention, finances, and support. Yet, only months before Eliot's speech, the Atlas Athletic Club had left the YMHA because, as Atlas president Lang, who served on the AAU's Metropolitan Basketball Committee during the mid-1900s, explained: "the fostering of athletics, with the hope that some day might see Jewish athletes gain recognition and merit (as Jews have done in other fields of life) has been the goal we have been striving to attain." Lang lamented "the inability of the Association" to support this goal even as "we have held together in the Association, hoping that some day the hand of fortune might shower on you to enable you to augment Jewish athletic prowess." Despite Lang's complaint regarding the YMHA's "inability" to provide financial support for athletic specialization, unwillingness may have been a more fitting word. Atlas's hope for a YMHA athletic culture had produced no appeal to "philanthropists," as YMHA officials remained silent regarding Atlas's departure. The YMHA had supported, ideologically if not financially, Atlas's desire to produce Jewish athletes; but prior to Eliot's comments, the YMHA had sought to avoid any engagement with the stereotype of the non-athletic, weak Jew. Yet, the institutional response to Eliot indicated the strength of the stereotype at a time when the question of Jewish physical regeneration had important implications regarding Jews' place in American society. Interestingly, the model of winning athletic honors in order to challenge future charges of Jewish physical weakness had been voiced only months earlier in the YMHA *Bulletin*.

In April 1907, an editorial had elucidated what would become the dominant paradigm about Jewish athleticism during the first half of the twentieth century. "The Jew as an Athlete" presented a familiar narrative: "Jews as a nation have never been actively identified with the manly sports, either in ancient or modern times." The Jews could be partially blamed for this absence. "Had the manly sports been more indulged . . . the Jews might have been treated with greater respect by their enemies." In the United States, "more attention is being paid by the Jews to the harmonious development of the human form and as a result, we are gradually developing a number of promising Jewish athletes." The editorial praised the public school system for helping produce successful athletes, especially in the "game of basket-ball, [where] Jewish young men are acknowledged leaders." Sports needed to become more important to Jewish "peoplehood," but with one important caveat. "There is something in athletics which appeals to all manly men and if the Jews will pay more attention to it and through it develop a number of champions, it will do more to raise the status of the race in the eyes of the world than any other single achievement."

The editorial demanded change in the relationship between American-Jewish culture and sports and constructed a new model of Jewish athleticism. Published one month after the Atlas Athletic Club left the YMHA (and possibly as a response to this development) and eight months before Eliot spoke before the Menorah Club, the editorial provided a model through which YMHA officials could respond to the Eliot controversy. The absence of "manly sports" within Jewish culture had served as a barrier to Jewish integration. Thus, individual Jews could benefit, if Jewish culture moved closer to sports. Mainstream society would accept Jews and provide a space for modern and normal manhood only if Jewish "champions" proved their worth in the athletic world. Expressed as an abstract and theoretical idea, this "champion-model" would eventually encourage the development of a communal athletic culture that could serve both as an external project, verifying to the outside world of the validity of Jewish athleticism and equally importantly, as an internal project, serving as a means of Jewish socialization into American culture.

In 1912, the champion-model's concept of competitive Jewish athleticism was adopted by New York area YMHAs with the formation of the YMHA Athletic League. The league's competitiveness encouraged member institutions to develop the hierarchical structures that would support an athletic club culture. Commitment is needed for competitive structures to succeed, and organized rules, governance, and scheduling meant the league privileged elite specialization in sports over mass participation. At the 92nd Street YMHA, internal competitions and tournaments between house and club teams expanded the pool from which representative teams could draw talent. Intra-association teams swelled from thirty in 1910 to more than fifty in 1915, and representative teams played against athletic clubs, public schools, YMCAs, settlements, and even the occasional college team ("Gymnastic Notes").[8] All of this activity served the Association's participation in the YMHA League, which limited participation to "only five regular players and a few substitutes [who] can represent us *directly* on the field." Members, however, could "represent us *indirectly* by their presence," at games as attendance became a "duty" and "organized rooting" encouraged the team to victory. At the end of the first season, the 92nd Street YMHA captured the league title in front of "an average attendance of 150 visitors" (Editorial, *Y Bulletin*; "YMHA Athletics").

Soon after the formation of the Athletic League, basketball at the 92nd Street YMHA became not only an athletic but also a financial endeavor. In 1914, the *Bulletin* explained: "Athletics should be self-supporting. We have the opportunity to make it so by attending the basketball games . . . every cent taken in at these games goes to encourage track and field sports and baseball, as well as basketball itself." During the 1910s, basketball's financial success allowed the YMHA to develop boxing, handball, and swimming programs ("Basketball").[9] The popularity of the 92nd Street YMHA basketball team led to expanded coverage in the *Bulletin* and an "Athletic News" column reported on star players and representative teams as they competed against a vast array of amateur and college teams, succeeded in AAU tournaments, and won league championships. At the same time, however, both the YMHA League and its member institutions banned Saturday play, which indicated that officials believed Jewish athletic culture could function adequately on a six-day athletic week and needed to pay heed to Jewish law and tradition. Yet, some young Jews found the official separation of Jewish athleticism from mainstream sports unsatisfactory, and this quickly led to tensions.

In July 1915, 92nd Street YMHA President Felix Warburg wrote a letter to physical director George Schoening, in which he explained that a few members had ingeniously "formed themselves into the so-called Manhattan Club, making it appear by using the cut of our building, that the same was their club-house." They did this in order to "play in competition on Saturdays, which the Board had ruled should not be permitted." Writing on behalf of the Board of Directors, Warburg communicated their concerns regarding "the attitude of our young men toward athletics." Besides the Sabbath incident, which officials never fully confronted in either private meetings or public declarations, he spelled out two other matters that needed to be addressed—gambling and professionalism. Competition could be a healthy activity for "our young men, handicapped as a good many of them are by generations of ancestors who have been forced to live in unhealthy surrounding and crowded districts." The YMHA needed to refocus its efforts toward fair play and sportsmanship since "the desire to excel and to win prizes has led us to give an undue importance to those young men who may turn out to be the winners." Placing blame squarely on themselves, YMHA directors and officials "feel that we may have been guilty of driving them forward in these ambitions, rather than warning them to improve their standing all around and thus causing them to specialize to a dangerous degree to the detriment to other boys, whom they have crowded out." Warburg appealed to Schoening to teach and develop "the ethics of sport . . . rather than the muscles alone."

The YMHA's directors, once again, found themselves on the horns of a dilemma—caught between their pragmatic desire to pursue the champion-model and their equally strong desire to preserve a more idealistic vision of what sports should be. The *Bulletin*'s 1907 call for champions had assumed competitive sports would be easily incorporated into American-Jewish culture. When confronted with the consequences of competitive sports, YMHA officials became determined to rein in their champions, although neither Warburg nor other YMHA officials contemplated abolishing competition.[10] Instead, the YMHA formed an official Athletic Committee in 1917 to replace an informal committee that possessed no authority to control members' actions, since it focused solely on financial matters.[11] Both directors and members governed the new Committee. Indeed, the first official committee to include members, it sought to protect the YMHA's growing reputation in mainstream sports. New YMHA President Irving Lehman placed the responsibility for developing "clean" sports in the hands of the members. At the committee's opening meeting, Lehman stated: "This is an experiment. If this experiment fails it hurts the kind of work in which you are especially interested ... pick out the kind of men [i.e., Committee members] who are going to stand for straight, clean athletics" ("Athletic Committee Re-Organized"). But before the Athletic Committee could produce results, America's entry into World War I caused the suspension of all YMHA League activities. The War's conclusion, however, saw the return of competitive basketball in a changing sports world for which Association officials found themselves ill prepared.

During the interwar period, American sports entered a new era. Athletic heroes such as Babe Ruth and Joe Louis were celebrated for their competitive accomplishments and made professionalism in sports more acceptable and indeed for many, highly admirable. The competitive and commercial environment of American sports impacted the structure of Jewish institutional basketball, as many athletes progressed from the junior level through intermediate onto the senior or varsity teams. The Philadelphia YMHA's physical director summarized his Center's program: "Each player on the [varsity] team coaches a team in the Inter-Fraternity League, which is made up of clubs.... The captains of these teams, in turn, coach the teams in the Junior League, and the same arrangement is maintained so that even 8 and 9-year-old boys are playing the same game in our gym under the guidance of the older and experienced boys" ("Basketball Team Excels"). Such a program existed within a broader culture in which the best Jewish players would compete for Jewish institutions and high school teams and then progress to college basketball. Often, players would move back and forth between professional and institutional basketball, thus continuing the culture of basketball champions within Jewish communities. For many officials at the 92nd Street YMHA and throughout the

Jewish institutional world, the problems associated with this basketball culture outweighed the positive aspects, as they struggled to produce a physical education program that avoided the pitfalls of competitive and commercial sports.

Immediately after the War, basketball games at the 92nd Street YMHA helped finance "Welcome Home" celebrations for returning veterans, as institutional membership grew to unprecedented numbers. Basketball also became the major source of revenue for the athletic department ("Athletic Notes"). A representative team called the Harmony Big Five played in front of capacity audiences and helped the physical department recover from a $28 deficit in 1919 to reach a budget surplus of just under $5,000 the following year (Athletic Committee records). But professionalism accompanied the commercial and competitive success of the Harmony team, and in October 1922, the YMHA Athletic Committee decided that, "members who engage in a sport professionally shall not be permitted to engage in the same sport in our gymnasium" (YMHA Athletic Committee, Minutes, Oct. 5, 1922). The following year, the YMHA denied Harmony the use of the gymnasium for practice and games because "it would be undesirable to have this team, which has been continuing to play professional ball, use our gymnasium for their training." The physical education department issued a memorandum against professionalism, but the YMHA did not expel Harmony players (repeating the exoneration of guilty athletes in the mid-1910s), and they eventually returned as the representative team, albeit in an amateur state (YMHA Athletic Committee, Minutes, Oct. 3, 1923; "Harmony's Victory in Harmony with Expectations").

In the mid-1920s, 92nd YMHA officials established a structure, in which management would control basketball, including player activity. Rather than allowing players to form a team that represented the institution, a coach would select a varsity team composed of the best players. The new model potentially restricted the sort of activity in which Harmony had engaged but did not decrease the commercial importance of basketball. In 1926, members formed the Athletic Council, which served as a representative body of gymnasium members, controlled its own activities and had a level of autonomy unseen elsewhere in the institution ("Athletic Council").[12] The following year, basketball coach "Spike" Spunberg criticized the YMHA membership for their lack of support at games and appealed to the Council rather than the board-controlled Athletic Committee. In response, the Council placed a representative on the Bulletin Committee to "guarantee the proper representation." In December 1929, the Council took over total control of the business management of varsity basketball and abolished free admission to any game (YMHA Athletic Committee,

Minutes, October 1927). The Council's desire to determine the direction of YMHA athletics necessitated financial autonomy from the Board of Directors, even as they worked together toward common institutional goals.

Similar to the 92nd Street YMHA, the YMHA League evolved during the 1920s. Re-named the Metropolitan League to take into consideration its representation of non-YMHA institutions, the league's expansion in the 1920s reflected the changing demographic patterns of New York Jews. Economic prosperity had allowed Jews to leave the lower East Side, and by 1925, only fifteen percent of New York Jews remained in the immigrant neighborhood (Wenger 83). The migration to the Bronx and Brooklyn made communal contact among Jews more tenuous and Jewish institutions attempted to fill the void caused by the dispersal. By the mid-1920s, sports served as the "principal means of establishing cordial relations between the members of the YMHA's in the Metropolitan district" ("1925—Its History, Aims, and Plans"; Leff, Letter to Nadel, April 19, 1925; Metropolitan League).[13] The league formed an Athletic Committee to control member behavior, standardize rules and regulations, and encourage league competition by awarding cups and trophies. Minutes of the league's various committees reveal a considerable amount of time spent ruling on the validity of team protests, the suspension and reinstatement of players, the standardization of rules, referees' decisions, and decisions regarding awards, trophies, and other minutia. The Metropolitan League also confronted gambling, which it banned at all events:

> No man who has been found guilty of placing or attempting to place a bet or acted as an agent for others in betting on athletic contests in the Metropolitan League shall be eligible to represent a constituent organization in any League activity [until] one year from the date of the occurrence of the act. The Board of Directors of the organization of which he is a member is to be notified and requested to take similar action. ("Report on Minimum Standards")

The wording of the ban indicated the normality of such activity within YMHA sports and the mention of agents meant players themselves may have participated in gambling activities. More pressing as an issue seemed to be professionalism, and during the early and mid-1920s, Metropolitan League officials had frequent discussions regarding the professional status of individual players. The league's Athletic Committee declared: "No man who has ever competed as a professional shall be eligible to play in this League." The committee generally gave institutions the benefit of the doubt regarding their ignorance of a player's professional standing, but the sheer volume of incidents indicated that institutional control and supervision were often lacking. As a result, the 92nd Street YMHA's Athletic Committee "went on record disapproving any YMHA giving out free athletic membership as an inducement to enroll athletes" ("Report on Minimum Standards."[14]

The perceived danger of unrestrained competitiveness caused officials at the 92nd Street YMHA to remind members that physical activity had more tangible benefits. Throughout the decade, numerous "health" articles appeared in the *Bulletin*, expressing sentiments that "physical training is not indicated merely for the making of athletes . . . but for the harmonious development of manhood in general" ("Physical Training"). In 1925, the department issued a memorandum which stated that the Association sought "to develop the highest type of virile manhood," while giving "members a better understanding of the Jewish faith" because "neuro-muscle habits play a very important part in the development of character." This memorandum indicated that athletic tournaments remained central to the organized department because "athletics, when wisely directed . . . [serve as] a means of development of character through self-control, temperate living, and fair play" ("Policy of the Department of Physical Education"). By connecting physical and character development with virile manhood and a sense of Jewishness, the YMHA hoped to mold Jewish youth who, it was feared, were otherwise being influenced by American society in unhealthy ways. Thus, the Association remained idealistically determined that the emerging American Jewish identity of young members should remain aligned with an ideology of pure sports, character, and "the right kind of manhood." In doing so, Association leaders continued to try to restrain the specialization encouraged by competitive sports.

At the center of this concept of communal Jewish athleticism, the Jewish Welfare Board (JWB) sought to construct a national Jewish Center movement to control previously independent YMHAs and JCCs. Historian David Kaufman has noted that officials founded the Center-movement based on the belief that "Jewish religious life was obsolete" and needed "to be replaced by the cultural and ethnic Jewishness of the secular center" (279). JWB educators and officials accepted the stereotype that traditional Jewish culture opposed physical activity and blamed religious leaders for neglecting physical activity, thus producing the weak Jewish physical body. The JWB was determined to correct this abnormality by rededicating itself to the idealistic model of what athleticism was supposed to be. In doing so, JWB officials attempted to contend with the champion-model in three ways. First, they denigrated institutional sports as containing the harmful "evils" associated with college athletics. Second, they constructed a Jewish physical education program that could be incorporated into the modern, Jewish culture advocated by the JWB. Finally, they conceptualized Jewish athleticism as appealing to the value of recreation for *all* institutional members, not just top athletes, the champions.

In October 1922, in the first issue of the JWB's *Jewish Center*, officials began their attack on the champion-model by hearkening back to rhetoric employed when athletics was first organized at the 92nd Street YMHA. Competition became dangerous "when the object becomes winning at any cost. Rather than lose, unfair practices may be resorted to by players or winked at by managers. Ineligible contestants may then be introduced. . . . [T]he outcome is a decline in sportsmanship, which is the flower of civilized play." Four years later, Newark executive director Aaron Robison denounced the elitist athletic structure that encouraged "aggressive self-assertion," which he believed "Jewish life now suffers too much from" (London; Robison 49). In June of that year, Abraham Rosenthal, the executive director of the Bronx YMHA, examined physical education at YMHAs and JCCs and stated that basketball:

> is responsible for every evil in a Jewish Center attributed to football and baseball in intercollegiate competition. Despite every effort to submerge the star player, to prevent betting and interference with the more important work of the gymnasium, a representative team in outside competition, in proportion to the number of games it wins, [gains] a cumulative, hectic interest on the part of a large number of our young people as worshipful spectators. (Rosenthal 42)[15]

The attack on Center basketball occurred because the champion-model had become defined by the competitive and commercial behavior that had become a standard in American sporting culture. The champion-model had been constructed to facilitate integration through communal involvement in the "manly" sports—but, from the standpoint of the JWB, it had accomplished its goal all too well.

In 1930, Samuel Leff, field secretary of the JWB, produced the most direct criticism on competitive sports published in the *Jewish Center*. He explained that the champion athlete had become harmful. "The silent, unspectacular large membership is the heart and soul of the gymnasium group, not the specialized teams. If we analyze impartially the sports situation in most Jewish Centers as well as elsewhere in America, we find that we are suffering from useless hero worship of spectacular athletes . . . at the expense of a physically, undeveloped mass of people." Leff also believed that, "Jewish values" had been "neglected" in the gymnasium or even "destructively mistaught." Competitive sports had led to "the intense and often savage fight for athletic victory." Leff explained that, "physical education in a Center must be judged by the universality of its use and not by the false, but unfortunately intrenched [sic] standard of championship teams composed of a small number of specially trained athletes." Leff singled out basketball as a sport containing "17 character values" that could be expressed in positive or negative ways, including "cooperation or the lack of it, self-control or the opposite, loyalty or disloyalty, etc." He admitted that members enjoyed playing and watching the sport, but "the disadvantages far outweigh the benefits." Basketball monopolized the gymnasium as a "fatiguing game" suited only for the young and demanded too much time from physical directors, who then neglected the larger membership. Leff condemned the "exaggerated emphasis on basket ball in many of our Jewish Centers" and suggested that "if the overemphasis on this sport cannot be curbed, I would favor its gradual elimination from all our Jewish Centers" (Leff, "Health and Physical Education").

It is not without irony that JWB's call for universal physical education to be favored over athletic elitism emerged from out of the same milieu that had originally encouraged the construction of the champion-model. Leff prevailed upon Jewish Centers to help Jews "overcome a measure of their ancestral tradition of over emphasis on mental development," and believed physical education could serve as a preventive measure since "physical defects are prevalent among members." JWB physical education would improve the Jewish body and Leff argued the ideal Jew would use the gymnasium "as an important medium for mental, moral, and spiritual development necessary in the well-balanced all-around, trained Jewish personality." JWB officials believed that "recreational activity in the Center is an educational process," and defended their use of recreation and physical education in comparison to the "more limited scope of formal Jewish activities." It had become necessary to include "social and athletic activities to impart interests that one may continue through life and not consider merely those that require youthful vigor and agility." Physical education at the Jewish Center would attract *all* Jews to the Center as an activity that encompassed the lifespan of American Jews and helped "develop the Jewish consciousness" (Kraft; Leff, "Health and Physical Education"; Robison 49). Leff expressed the JWB hope to connect sports to the organization's attempts to mold Jewish youth along character building principles. Still, not surprisingly, the JWB had difficulty controlling competitive sports at Jewish centers because many, including the 92nd Street YMHA, structured their entire physical education departments around the champion-model.

In the 1930s, as the role of athletics continued to be hotly debated, officials, who hoped to prevail over the competitive athletic culture, found an unlikely ally in one of the era's greatest professional players and college coach, Nat Holman. In the spring of 1930, the 92nd Street YMHA moved into a new, modern building and hired Holman as their director of physical education. He retired from professional basketball to take the position, although he continued to coach at the City College of New York (CCNY). Holman's eight-year tenure reflected the Center's struggle for athletic balance. Despite his own professional basketball career, Holman unrelentingly promoted mass participation over varsity athletics in his new position, stating, "the super-athlete is not our goal but one wherein those interested in our activities will develop a fair amount of skill so that he can obtain a reasonable amount of enjoyment from actual participation" (Holman, "Monthly Report of the Physical Director"). A little more than one year into his appointment, Holman condemned competitive basketball. In September 1931, Holman suggested abolishing the Metropolitan League because "the effects of institutional basketball are not to be found by studying the game, but by studying the spirit of the institution." He stated that:

> Winning basketball teams are sometimes necessary evils among certain institutions to attract new members to the building; possibly the incoming revenue from these games covers the expenses incurred by other sports. The question centers around [sic] control. Visiting or home teams who bring their enthusiasts along to bet on games in a most unscrupulous manner, to question every decision of the officials, to desire to win at any price by the players and coaches; to deliberately employ unfair tactics in order to get a star player out of the game, to boo at the time an opponent is shooting a foul—make for a very unwholesome influence in our Jewish centers.

Holman discussed pervasive problems associated with Center basketball. Betting, booing, arguing, and excessive competitiveness had no place in organized Jewish communal life. Rather, sports should "uphold all the ideals and principles of clean sportsmanship, honesty, and fair play." Expanding on these points at considerable length, Holman concluded by reiterating his objective: "we have got to consider the interest of the mass rather than any specialized few" ("Holman Suggests Abolition of Met. League Basketball").

The article sparked considerable discussion. In mid-October, the YMHA Athletic Committee studied the "defects" of the league's basketball competition, including "bitter feeling among the Associations, disorder, gambling, and other vices." Holman's proposal faced strong opposition from Committee members, who voted that the Association should remain in the league to ensure "better spirit and closer supervision" (Athletic Committee, Minutes, October 13, 1931). One week later, the Metropolitan League's Physical Director's Society discussed how "the element of championship had stimulated excessive rivalry." They concluded that an "over-emphasis upon basketball," had led to "unsportsmanlike situations." The directors commented on the difficulty of controlling the "attitudes of the spectators" due to the established rivalries. They decided that if Centers played each other less often, the tensions involved in bitter contests would decline. League competition would be organized into three divisions "in such a manner that each association will rotate in relation to its competitors from one year to another" (Physical Directors Society, Minutes).

Interestingly, Leff, who had condemned Center basketball in the *Jewish Center* the previous year, proved to be one of the most adamant opponents of Holman's proposal. He believed that Holman misunderstood the situation. He agreed that "evils" plagued the league, but "these faults are not inherent in the league." Rather, they "are foreign growths that have attached themselves to league games. These growths can be removed by stricter regulations." Leff believed his long-time association with the league allowed for a more accurate assessment of the situation. He explained: "merely because some of the organizations or to be more exact, some of the players representing some YMHA's display very bitter and unsportsmanlike feelings and conduct toward one another, there is no reason to abolish the league." He added that "similarly, there is no justification for ending the leagues because of any betting that may go on by members or other spectators at the games." The league controlled institutional actions and its abolition would mean that, "no standing of eligibility would exist and high school players, college players, professionals and even 'ringers' would be brought in to win important games. There would also be a great temptation to professionalize the sport by paying good players" ("Leff Expresses Disagreement with Nat Holman's Views").

Metropolitan League officials bickered among themselves about the future of Center basketball. Leff suggested abolishing tournaments during this controversy because, "competitive tournaments have interfered with sound development of physical education in Jewish Centers." He pointed to the Bensonhurst Jewish Community House, which "abolished all varsity teams," and found "membership interest and participation in intra-association athletics is at its highest point in the history of the organization." Powerful league officials opposed Leff. Charles Ornstein, a future member of the US Olympic Committee, believed abolishment would "stifle competitive sports within the YMHA." E. J. Londow agreed, and explained that "the difficulty lies in the fact that the activity had been put in the hands of professionals [coaches], whose main interest lay in a winning record of their teams." Rosenthal went so far as to suggest the league should appoint a basketball commissioner to standardize the "dissimilarity of membership standards," which had been caused by the "employment of professional talent for Jewish center basketball teams, due to the need for money to carry out the organizations' physical education program" ("Met League Abolishes All Athletic Tournaments").

In October 1933, Metropolitan League officials declared a "one-year moratorium" on all athletic tournaments. The league's Athletic, Health, and Physical Education Committee appointed Judge Aron Steuer to head a subcommittee that would investigate "whether tournament competition is the basic cause of the unpleasantness or if the fault lies in curable defects in the administration of these tournaments" ("Met League Abolishes All Athletic Tournaments"). Leff supported the decision. His reversal on the abolishment of tournaments would seem curious if not for the fact that he often acted as an arbiter of athletic activities and expected his opinion to steer the direction of Center athletics. Correspondence between Leff and 92nd Street YMHA officials, especially executive director Jack Nadel, was cordial and friendly, but often contained an underlying tension. This tension surfaced during a controversy over YMHA basketball in 1933.

At roughly the same time as the formation of the Steuer Committee, the 92nd Street YMHA's Athletic Council went on record that the YMHA would not play professionals. It cancelled its regular season opener against the Harlem Rens, an all-black team considered one of the best professional teams of the era. The Council soon reversed its position on a technicality, however, because the opening game "was not a contest but an exhibition." The Council decided that since the game would be "held for revenue only, in order to outfit the team properly," it found no problem with scheduling "against a team that would be the most certain to bring us the needed revenue." Besides, as the Council further noted, a poorly attended first game "would surely lower the attendance for the remainder of the season." The Council then scheduled a professional team, the Original Celtics (Nat Holman's old team) in order to "insure a large crowd for the opening contest." The Council's president told the *Bulletin*, however, that in the future, "the 'no-professional' policy will be adhered to" (Athletic Council, Minutes, Sept. 14, 1933; Athletic Council, Minutes, Oct. 10, 1933).

The Celtics game blatantly violated amateur rules. The YMHA received a letter from the AAU demanding an explanation, and Leff, who had reported the YMHA's actions to the AAU, asked officials to clarify "the present policy of your YMHA" in relation to "such games with professionals." Jack Nadel retorted: "we engage in competition with amateur teams only" (Banov; Leff, Correspondence with Nadel, Nov. 6, 1933; Dec. 27, 1933; Dec. 29, 1933; Jan. 4, 1934). The following year, Leff returned to the subject upon learning that the YMHA had again scheduled games against professional teams, including the Harlem Rens. He demanded the YMHA stop playing against these teams since "there is danger that your team will be regarded as violating amateur rules, and the reputation of your organization in all amateur sports will likewise suffer." Leff appealed to the YMHA's importance within the Center movement. If the YMHA established a strict policy of amateurism to guarantee the "gradual elimination of any danger of professionalism," it would "set a high standard for the other YMHA's and Jewish Centers throughout the country" (Leff, Letter to Holman).

The Steuer Committee had blamed commercial incentives (such as the kind that would have produced games against professionals) for the "evils" of the Metropolitan League. The committee believed proper supervision would solve the problems and recommended that all Centers needed to organize athletic councils "to finance and supervise athletic activities" ("Met League Abolishes All Athletic Tournaments"). Experience indicated, however, that athletic councils would focus on the financial rather than the supervisory aspects of the games. At the 92nd Street YMHA, the Athletic Council relied on the basketball program to fund the entire athletic department. Between July 1931 and January 1933, income from basketball games constituted ninety-eight percent of the total revenue of the Athletic Council. In 1935, receipts from basketball games reached over $4,000 and the "net receipts" generated more than $1,500. Two years later, the basketball team averaged 530 spectators per game and generated almost $2,000 in revenue, an especially impressive sum during the Depression.[16]

The continued commercialism of Jewish Center sports did not stop the Steuer Committee from recommending in May 1935 that the Metropolitan League resume basketball tournaments after a two-year absence. The following year, the Metropolitan League incorporated as the New York Metropolitan Section-JWB, Inc. ("Metropolitan League Plans to Restore Competitive Tournaments"). Neither development immediately changed the priorities of Centers in the Metropolitan League, which contained approximately thirty-five member institutions spread throughout New York City, New Jersey, Long Island, and Westchester County. Competitive basketball at the 92nd Street YMHA flourished as former college players from LIU, St. John's, Brooklyn College, and even Minnesota starred for the team. The Athletic Council continued to encourage a competitive and commercial culture. The Council formed a Varsity Club to reward the best athletes in 1936 and began granting an annual Outstanding Athlete Award the following year (Board of Directors, YMHA, Minutes, November 16, 1937). Through the end of the decade, the YMHA played the top amateur teams in New York City, regular competition in the Metropolitan League, and replaced professional opponents with College All-Star teams until the AAU forbade them to do so.

In September 1939, the 92nd Street YMHA's Athletic Council agreed to participate in a JWB national basketball tournament, hailed as the first attempt at a national sports competition. According to the *Bulletin*, officials designed the new tournament to "further the concept of the Jewish Center movement as a national movement, to enable Jews to find points of contact with Jews everywhere, and to further Jewishness, generally." Officials regarded basketball as "the most popular sport of Jewish youth," and believed the tournament would serve as the catalyst for future athletic events to strengthen and coordinate American Jewry ("To Unite Jewry Aim of JWB Sports Plan").

Like the initial YMHA Athletic League, the JWB hoped to use sports to strengthen internal communal forces. Unlike the original league, however, the JWB did not intend to promote Jewish athleticism—despite the continued strength of the stereotype of the weak, unathletic Jew. In the run-up to the 1936 Berlin (Nazi) Olympics, General Charles Sherrill, a member of the International Olympic Committee, had stated that, "it was not easy to get a good Jewish athlete" and "there was never a prominent Jewish athlete in history" ("A General Warns Jews to Lay Low or Else"). In response, the Jewish press condemned Sherrill, and Jewish sportswriter Stanley Frank wrote an expansive book on Jewish athleticism called *The Jew in Sports*. While Sherrill may have elicited some of the anxiety reminiscent of that Eliot's comments had produced in 1907, Frank's book reflected the general success of the champion-model. At the institutional level, however, neither the YMHA nor the JWB responded to Sherrill with a renewed call for champions. The institutional structure no longer served the purpose of diffusing the stereotype, since Jews had started to integrate through the use of sports and other American activities. Whether fully recognized at the time or not, the era of Jewish communal institutions organizing athletic contests to disprove the stereotype had come to an end.

The 1907 *Bulletin* editorial had been written as a theoretical and abstract concept of Jewish athleticism. When applied, officials at the 92nd Street YMHA, other institutions, and perhaps most importantly, the JWB, had found that elite athleticism produced negatives that, from their idealistic perspective, clearly outweighed any positives. By the end of the 1930s, the JWB tournament and the reorganized Metropolitan League (now called the Eastern Jewish Center League) included many of the rules that had governed previous tournaments and competitions. Yet, the organizational structure and supervision had become far more extensive with committees for referees, scheduling, and rules ("Meeting of Representatives"). Perhaps most damaging to the champion-model, the rules committee stipulated that players be members of the organizations they represented and could not play for any other organization, including colleges. Officials believed this rule would "eliminate 'professionalism' from Jewish Center sports" ("To Unite Jewry Aim of JWB Sports Plan"). The JWB intended to drive commercialism and intense competitiveness out of Center basketball. Its success occurred quicker and more definitively than officials could have dared hoped.

During the 1937 season, the 92nd Street YMHA reached a record level in both attendance, an average of 534 fans, and income, netting an average of $104.37 per game. Two years later, the Athletic Council found itself in the midst of a budget crisis because the revenue from basketball had declined to an average of just $56.89 per game. In 1940, basketball had for one year a slight revival, as the average net receipts increased to $85 per game, but this aberration did not change the depressed state of YMHA basketball. Attendance hovered around an average of 400 fans per game and expenses held steady at $100 per game, but receipts declined during the 1941 season, when basketball netted an average of only $51.49 per game. The sudden decline in revenue surprised the athletic department and in 1941, the Athletic Council requested funds from the board to cover the expenses of all varsity teams for the first time since the early 1920s (Athletic Council files).

Prior to the 1942 season, board members took a close look at the Athletic Council's budget and financial figures and issued a report entitled "Basketball at the 92nd Street YMHA." The board examined the structure of the team, including the coach's role in selecting players and purchasing equipment. The majority of the report focused on the commercial side: "The money realized from these games, [is] our only source of revenue." They needed this revenue "to equip and finance all other varsity teams," pay AAU dues and "for contributions" to a summer camp and other charitable causes. The report blamed the lack of revenue on a number of factors, but reserved special mention for the "poor competition" of the JWB tournament since "some of the teams are not attractive to our patrons. They have no following and hence do not bring a crowd with them. Our games must necessarily be a money proposition." It recommended that the YMHA needed to play "only the best competition, get a winning team, [and] start the season against a team of stars" ("Basketball at the 92nd Street YMHA, 1941-1942").

America's entry into World War II made it impossible for the report's recommendations to be implemented. The depletion of Association resources caused the 92nd Street YMHA to cancel all varsity sports. During the War, the New York Young Women's Hebrew Association (YWHA) moved into the YMHA after giving up its building to the army, and in 1945, the institution reorganized as the 92nd Street YM-YWHA. The transformation of the YMHA symbolized the emergence of a new form of Jewish community center (Borish, "An Interest in Physical Well-Being" 92-93). While college and professional basketball would help create a new era of modern sporting culture in American society, the suburbanization of American Jewry finalized the decline of the champion-model. Voluntary Jewish identification became part of suburban life and the suburban Jewish Center needed to fill a void left by the declining Jewish urban neighborhoods (Shapiro, Preface; Feingold 125). The post-war Center would provide cultural activities in which an ethnic identity could be constructed (Kaufman 235). It did not need competitive Jewish athleticism. Physical education at this new JCC would be recreational, although even this conception of Jewish athleticism had its detractors.

In 1948, the JWB issued the *JWB Survey*, also known as the Janowsky Report after its chair Oscar Janowsky, which concluded that Jewish Centers needed to "Judaize" their programs. Religious leaders had claimed that the Jewish Center "made only 'some' or no major contribution towards the furtherance of Judaism." JWB officials such as Louis Kraft continued to assert that Centers, as social, religious, and cultural institutions, helped "our youth live affirmatively as Jews." Janowsky believed, however, that the focus on recreational activities needed to be diminished. "It is not the gymnasium and dance hall that validate the distinctive Jewish Center, but its Jewish purpose ... American Jewry is neither an athletic association, nor a health club, nor a dancing society, nor even a recreational fraternity, however, broadly one defines recreation" (Gurock 103). The Janowsky Report, which went further than Kraft or other JWB officials in denouncing athletic activity in Jewish centers, reinforced the notion that competitive sports no longer had a place in the JWB. Thus, the champion-model had been effectively removed from organized American Jewish life.

YMHA basketball never recovered from its wartime decline. In 1946, the Athletic Council sought to resume varsity sports and appealed for over $2,000 from the Board of Directors, half of which would be used to revitalize basketball. In 1947, the net receipts from basketball were less than $600, one-quarter of the amount raised in 1935 (Athletic Council, Minutes, Oct. 1946).[17] Two years later, the YMHA played the Montreal YMHA, whose players composed half of Canada's 1948 Olympic basketball team, as part of the YMHA's 75th Anniversary celebration. This international competition aside, a *Bulletin* article the previous year indicated the true state of YMHA basketball and competitive sports in general. "Noted Sports Stars Listed Among Y's Membership" listed past athletes and possessed a nostalgic tone of recollection rather than hope for future success. At the end of the decade, because of "injuries, illnesses, and players getting married, the Varsity basketball team had its poorest season in Y history" ("Noted Sports Stars"; "Montreal Game to Climax One of Y's Best Seasons"). Varsity teams would continue to play, but they would no longer play in front of large audiences and rarely included future or former college stars. The JWB's success in controlling Jewish center sports had impacted basketball at the 92nd Street YMHA and thus hastened its demise.

During an era when American Jews celebrated baseball slugger Hank Greenberg, boxing champion Benny Leonard, football legend Benny Friedman, and basketball star Nat Holman, the JWB had dismantled a competitive athletic culture that had been created to produce *more* of these sporting champions. Jewish educators believed that competitive sports had become a dangerous activity, and that competitive basketball, in particular, should not be made an integral part of modern American Jewish culture. Center officials firmly believed that, during the interwar period, players, and fans had participated in too many unscrupulous activities that accompanied competitive sports: capitalistic and aggressive behavior. Thus, the JWB withdrew from this form of Jewish athleticism and made every effort to connect Jewish manhood (through sports) with mass as opposed to elite participation. The champion-model was based on the notion that sports could serve a process of integration. But once Jews believed that sports had achieved this particular end, they further believed it could be transformed into a purely recreational activity whose sole purpose should be to unify American Jews. But this idealistic approach ignored a basic fact about what draws people (Jewish and non-Jewish) to sports: the celebration of exceptionalism, the capacity of given individuals to accomplish athletic feats that the rest of us can only cheer from the stands. Such sports elitism always needs a place and sufficient time in which to develop. But the post-World War II generation of Jewish players would find an important pathway to this highly competitive basketball world closed in their faces. If a young Jewish player from New York wanted to play college basketball, he could no longer rely on a Jewish Center to provide a competitive outlet. Future Jewish champions might succeed in sports, but they would have to compete as individuals, not as evidence of communal athleticism or as part of a communal Jewish culture. The result was nothing less than the transformation of American Jewish athleticism. Ironically, in trying to make sports more egalitarian and broad based and less "cut-throat" competitive—thereby giving the lie to the stereotype of the physically weak Jew—the 92nd Street YMHA, its related institutions and supporters, ended up undercutting their own athletic culture and marginalizing Jewish basketball.

Notes

1. Cf. James Naismith, the inventor of basketball ("Basket Ball").
2. In December 1935, for example, *Newsweek* declared that basketball was "a sport at which Jews excel." See "Basketball: Peach Basket Soccer Goes on the Big Time."
3. For the formation of the athletic club, also see "William Mitchell Journal," September 3, 1898. In the late 1890s, institutional leaders initiated an annual fee for gymnasium members and hired a permanent gymnasium instructor. On the gymnasium, see the New York Young Men's Hebrew Association, *Twenty-Fifth Annual Report, 1899*. Also see the Board of Directors, YMHA, "Minutes," January–October 1898. Among the moves made by the directors was the addition of gymnastic apparatus, such as a horizontal bar and a medicine ball. The instructor organized physical culture classes and gymnastic exhibitions in 1898.
4. On the establishment of country clubs among acculturated Jews, see Levine, "Our Crowd At Play." The country clubs formed by Jews, while they contained elite sports such as golf and tennis, served more as social rather than athletic institutions. The establishment of the country club is intimately connected to the increased social discrimination that acculturated Jews faced in the late nineteenth century. On social discrimination and immigration, see Higham 123–36. On anti-Semitism in American sports, see Jaher. The most famous example of individual Jews' participation in secular athletic clubs was Daniel Stern's involvement in the founding of the famous New York Athletic Club. The NYAC, however, became notorious for its exclusion of Jews.
5. For an example of the generalization that institutional leaders controlled sports, see "Sports & Immigrant Jews." According to the YMHA Board of Directors minute book, members petitioned to form a basketball team in October 1900. The best source for information on the YMHA's daily operations in the early 1900s is the "Daily Journal" of William Mitchell, the superintendent from 1898–1912. Mitchell noted in his journal on October 21, 1900 that the Executive Committee agreed to "add a complete Basket Ball team outfit to the Gym."
6. The January 1902 *YMHA Bulletin* explained that the final game occurred on December 18, 1901, because competition with outside teams, "interfere[s] too much with the regular work of the gymnasium." Mitchell's journal makes no mention of interference, but he noted that two YMHA players were injured in the December 18th game and that during an October game, one of the players "struck his head against the wall."
7. For the first mention of the YMHA's membership in the AAU, see Sperling. During its initial foray into basketball, therefore, YMHA had been on the outside of the official amateur structure. The YMHA would not have been considered a renegade, but it is nonetheless surprising that YMHA officials did not immediately conform to governing amateur rules in order to avoid any pretense of controversy. Throughout

the late 1890s and early 1900s, the AAU found itself in the midst of controversies involving the registration policy. Problems were often intensified when a non-registered team played a registered team, which made the registered team ineligible for AAU membership. If that team then played others, all the teams would be considered non-registered and so on. For information and controversies regarding AAU sport, the use of registration fees, and the AAU's connection to commercial consumption, see Horger 76–79.

8. On the number of intra-association teams (teams that played within the institution} in 1910 as well as information on the Mohegans, discussed immediately below, see "Gymnastic Notes." On the number of teams in 1915, see "Athletic News". The YMHA used the term "representative" to describe any team that competed against outside teams. Most of the "representative" teams in the early 1900s were club teams that also competed in intra-association tournaments. The most successful team was the Mohegans, led by Lazarus Joseph, a player and coach at YMHA. Joseph played at NYU prior to joining the 92nd Street YMHA and was the grandson of Rabbi Jacob Joseph. The Mohegans and other "representative" teams occasionally traveled to New Jersey to compete. In 1912, the Mohegans had a record of 25–1.

9. The statement regarding self-sufficiency indicates the desire that athletics not take funding away from other programming, and thus ensure the relative autonomy of the athletic department.

10. The incident appears to have resulted solely in a *Bulletin* article that praised YMHA athletes for not competing on the Sabbath. This article was written by a member of the Board of Directors, the Reverend Dr. Samuel Schulman. See "The Opportunities for the Jewish Character." Athletes guilty of gambling and professionalism were briefly suspended.

11. An example of praise awarded on the basketball team is found in the 1917 YMHA *Annual Report*, which proudly reported the 32–1 record of the team. The following year, the *Bulletin* editor and physical director picked an All-YMHA team from "in-house" teams. The existence of this all-star team is the best indication of a shifting ideology toward basketball, as honored players were chosen solely for "playing ability," and "points scored," with no mention of sportsmanship, moral value, or other progressive ideals. On the formation of the initial committee in 1913, see "Committee on Athletics."

12. Harry Henshel, Athletic Committee chairman, to prospective representatives. See Miscellaneous File. The first mention of the Council in the *Bulletin* was in "Athletic Council." The Council's original goal was to overcome overcrowding by bringing "members of the gymnasium in closer contact with each other." The Council was divided into representatives from "major" and "minor" sports. Basketball was declared a "major" sport along with baseball, track, and others. "Minor" sports included tennis, gymnastics, and handball. The Council also formed an Executive

Committee, which included the physical director, athletic coaches, the Athletic Committee chairman and elected gymnasium members.
13. The original YMHA Athletic League had member institutions in Westchester (Mt. Vernon and Yonkers), Brooklyn, and New Jersey (Bayonne and Perth Amboy).
14. A similar document titled "Athletic Committee Rules" was found in a miscellaneous folder titled "1922–26," Athletic Committee records. Athletic Committee, Minutes, September 22, 1924. The record of Minutes of the Athletic Committee are located in the Metropolitan League records, 92nd Street Y Archives, New York. Though not complete, the minutes provide a significant amount of detail regarding the internal workings of the league. For examples of rulings on the professional status of players, see January 9, 1923. In these minutes, the Committee ruled on establishing a reinstatement policy for professionals.
15. Rosenthal began the article by explaining that physical education "has reawakened a physical courage and a practical, cheerful idealism dormant for centuries . . . beautified and glorified the neglected physique of an entire race." The article was based on a questionnaire the JWB sent to institutions across the country. The questionnaire asked about gymnasium facilities, affiliations with summer camps, and athletic programs. The majority of respondents declared their facilities were "good" and three-fourths had "full-year, all-season [athletic] programs." Three centers "limit themselves to the competitive sport in which Jewish stars predominate—basketball."
16. Financial figures from miscellaneous Athletic Council files, Young Men's Hebrew Association records, 92nd Street Y Archives, New York. Much of the money raised went to charities and funds, including the Maccabi Association in Palestine, the Hebrew Orphan Asylum, the Jewish Federation, and the YMHA's special fund, Keren Ami (Fund for My People). What is important to note, however, is that these charities and funds were by-products of the revenue from basketball games and did not constitute the end goal for basketball. Most of the basketball revenue was used by the Athletic Council to benefit the athletic program rather than social programs or the broader institution.
17. Following the war, New York fire regulations limited the attendance at games to 200 spectators. See Athletic Council, Minutes, Oct. 1946. See miscellaneous Athletic Council files.

Works Cited

"1925—Its History, Aims, and Plans." Folder "1922–26, Metropolitan League Records." Young Men's Hebrew Association Records. 92nd Street Y Archives, New York [YMHA, 92nd Street Y Archives].

"A General Warns Jews to Lay Low or Else." *The American Hebrew* 25 Oct. 1935

"Are the Jews Really Inferior?" *Y Bulletin* Feb. 1908.

"Athletic Committee Re-Organized." *Y Bulletin* April 1917.

Athletic Committee, Metropolitan League. Minutes. 9 Jan. 1923. Metropolitan League Records. 92nd Street Y Archives, New York [ML, 92nd Street Y Archives].

———. Minutes. 22 Sept. 1924. ML, 92nd Street Y Archives.

———. Minutes. 13 Oct. 1931. ML, 92nd Street Y Archives.

Athletic Committee, YMHA. Minutes. 5 Oct 1922. YMHA, 92nd Street Y Archives.

———. Minutes. 3 Oct. 1923. YMHA, 92nd Street Y Archives.

———. Minutes. 3 Oct. 1923. YMHA, 92nd Street Y Archives.

———. Minutes. Oct. 1927. YMHA, 92nd Street Y Archives.

"Athletic Committee Rules." Folder "1922-26." Athletic Committee records, Young Men's Hebrew Association. 92nd Street Y Archives, New York.

Athletic Council Files. YMHA, 92nd Street Y Archives.

"Athletic Council." *Y Bulletin* 26 Nov. 1926.

Athletic Council, YMHA. Minutes. 14 Sept. 1933. YMHA, 92nd Street Y Archives.

———. Minutes. 10 Oct. 1933. YMHA, 92nd Street Y Archives.

———. Minutes. Oct. 1946. YMHA, 92nd Street Y Archives.

"Athletics in the YMHA." *YMHA Bulletin* Oct. 1908.

"Athletic News." *Y Bulletin* Dec. 1915.

"Athletic Notes." *Y Bulletin*. 28 Feb. 1919.

Banov, Ellis. Correspondence with the AAU registration chairman. 28–31 Oct. 1933. YMHA, 92nd Street Y Archives.

"Basketball." *Y Bulletin* Dec. 1914.

"Basketball: Peach Basket Soccer Goes on the Big Time." *Newsweek* 14 Dec. 1935.

"Basketball and Morals." *YMHA Bulletin* Dec. 1906.

"Basketball at the 92nd Street YMHA, 1941–1942." Miscellaneous Athletic Council file. YMHA, 92nd Street Y Archives.

"Basketball Team Excels." *Philadelphia Jewish Times* 20 Dec. 1927.

Board of Directors, YMHA. "Minutes." June 1893–Jan. 1898. YMHA, 92nd Street Y Archives.

———. Minutes. Jan.–Oct. 1898. YMHA, 92nd Street Y Archives.

———. Minutes. 16 Nov. 1937. YMHA, 92nd Street Y Archives.

Borish. Linda J. " 'An Interest in Physical Well-Being Among the Female Membership': Sporting Activities for Women the Young Men's and Young Women's Hebrew Associations." *American Jewish History* 87 (March 1999): 61–93.

"Committee on Athletics." *Y Bulletin*. April 1913.
Editorial. *Jewish Criterion* 27 Dec. 1907.
Editorial. *Jewish Outlook.*, 3 Jan. 1908.
Editorial. *Y Bulletin* Nov. 1912.
Feingold, Henry L. *A Time for Searching: Entering the Mainstream, 1920–1945.* Baltimore: Johns Hopkins Univ., 1992.
Frank, Stanley. *The Jew in Sports.* New York: Miles, 1936.
Gurock, Jeffrey S. *Judaism's Encounter with American Sports.* Bloomington: Indiana Univ., 2005.
"Gymnastic Notes." *Y Bulletin* Dec. 1909.
"Harmony's Victory in Harmony with Expectations." *Y Bulletin* 16 Oct. 1925.
Higham, John. *Send These To Me: Immigrants in Urban America.* Rev. ed. Baltimore: Johns Hopkins Univ., 1984.
Holman, Nat. "Monthly Report of the Physical Director." Oct. 1934. YMHA, 92nd Street Y Archives.
"Holman Suggests Abolition of Met. League Basketball." *Y Bulletin* 25 Sept. 1931.
Horger, Marc. "Play By The Rules: The Creation of Basketball and the Progressive Era, 1891–1917." Diss., Ohio State Univ., 2001.
Jaher, Frederic Cople. "Antisemitism in American Athletics." *Shofar* 20 (Fall 2001): 61–73.
Janowsky Report (*JWB Survey*). 1948. Jewish Welfare Board Records. 92nd Street Y Archives, New York [JWB, 92nd Street Y Archives].
"The Jew as an Athlete." *YMHA Bulletin* April 1907.
Jones, Oliver S. "Morality in College Athletics." *The North American Review* 160 (1 May 1895): 638–40.
Kaufman, David. *Shul with a Pool: The 'Synagogue Center' in American Jewish History.* Hanover, NH: Univ. of New England, 1999.
Kraft, Louis. "Proceedings of the 11th Annual Conference of National Association of Jewish Community Center Secretaries: Address of the President." *Jewish Center* 72 (June 1929).
Lang, Henry. Letter to YMHA Board of Directors. 20 March 1907. YMHA, 92nd Street Y Archives.
Leff, Samuel. Letter to Jack Nadel. 29 April 1925. Correspondence Files, ML, 92nd Street Y Archives.
———. Letter to Nat. Holman. 8 Oct. 1934. YMHA, 92nd Street Y Archives.
———. Correspondence with Jack Nadel. 6 Nov. 1933. Correspondence Files, JWB, 92nd Street Y Archives, Executive Director records.
———. Correspondence with Jack Nadel. 27 Dec. 1933. Correspondence Files, JWB, 92nd Street Y Archives, Executive Director records.
———. Correspondence with Jack Nadel. 29 Dec. 1933. Correspondence Files, JWB, 92nd Street Y Archives, Executive Director records.

———. Correspondence with Jack Nadel. 4 Jan. 1934. Correspondence Files, JWB, 92nd Street Y Archives, Executive Director records.

———. "Health and Physical Education in Jewish Community Centers." *Jewish Center* 1930.

"Leff Expresses Disagreement with Nat Holman's Views." *Y Bulletin* 2 Oct. 1931.

Levine, Peter. *Ellis Island to Ebbets Field: Sport and the American-Jewish Experience.* New York: Oxford Univ., 1992.

———. "Our Crowd At Play: The Elite Country Clubs in the 1920s." *Sports and the American Jew.* Ed. Steven A. Riess. *Sports and the American Jew.* Syracuse: Syracuse Univ., 1997. 160–81.

Londow, E. J. "Inter-Association Activities." *Jewish Center* 1.1 (Oct. 1922).

"Meeting of Representatives for the Formation of Invitational Basketball Tournaments of the Jewish Welfare Board Sports Programs." 1 Oct. 1939. JWB, 92nd Street Y Archives.

Mendes, H. Pereira. Letter to the President and Directors of the YMHA. 24 May 1890. YMHA, 92nd Street Y Archives.

"Met League Abolishes All Athletic Tournaments." *Y Bulletin* 20 Oct. 1933.

"Metropolitan League Plans to Restore Competitive Tournaments." *Y Bulletin* 3 May 1935.

Metropolitan League. "Metropolitan League of YMHAs to Extend Activities." Press release. 11 May 1925. ML, 92nd Street Y Archives.

Miscellaneous File. Physical Education department files. 6 Oct. 1926. YMHA, 92nd Street Y Archives.

"Montreal Game to Climax One of Y's Best Seasons." *Y Bulletin* 9 March 1949.

Naismith, James. "Basket Ball." *American Physical Education Review* 19.5 (May 1914): 339.

New York Young Men's Hebrew Association. *Twenty-Fifth Annual Report, 1899.* New York: 1900.

"Noted Sports Stars." *Y Bulletin* 15 Dec. 1948.

"The Opportunities for the Jewish Character." *Y Bulletin* May 1916.

Physical Directors Society. Minutes. 19 Oct. 1931. ML, 92nd Street Y Archives.

"Physical Training." *YMHA Bulletin* 22 Dec. 1922.

"Policy of the Department of Physical Education of the YMHA." YMHA, 92nd Street Y Archives.

"President Eliot at the Menorah Society." *Jewish Advocate* 27 Dec. 1907.

"Rabbi Chas. Fleischer's Reply to President Eliot." *Jewish Voice* 10 Jan. 1908.

"Rabbi Excerpts to Eliot Speech." *New York Times* 22 Dec. 1907: 14.

"The Recent Basketball Tournament." *Y Bulletin* May 1905.

"Report on Minimum Standards of Health Education Recommended by the Metropolitan League." ML, 92nd Street Y Archives.

Riess, Steven A., ed. *Sports and the American Jew.* Syracuse: Syracuse Univ., 1997.

Robison, Aaron G. "Physical Education in the Jewish Community Center (Discussion)." *Jewish Center* 4.3 (June 1926): 49.

Rosenthal, Abraham W. "Physical Education in the Jewish Community Center: In Relation to the Entire Program of the Jewish Center." *Jewish Center* 4.3 (June 1926): 42.

Shapiro, Edward S. *A Time for Healing: American Jewry Since World War II*. Baltimore: Johns Hopkins Univ., 1992.

Sperling, Harry. "Gymnasium Notes." *YMHA Bulletin* Dec. 1903.

"Sports & Immigrant Jews." *MyJewishLearning.com*. N.d. 22 Aug. 2014 <http://www.myjewishlearning.com/culture/2/Sports/Sports_and_Judaism/America.shtml?p=0>.

"To Unite Jewry Aim of JWB Sports Plan." *Y Bulletin* 6 Oct. 1939.

Townsend, George Alfred. "Recreations of Eminent Men." *The Chatauquan* 15 (August 1892): 582–88.

Turner, Charles. "Golf in Gotham." *Outing* 34 (1899): 443–57.

"Urges Jews to be Strong." *New York Times* 21 Dec. 1907.

Warburg, Felix. Letter to George Schoening. 26 July 1915. YMHA, 92nd Street Y Archives.

Wenger, Beth S. *New York Jews and the Great Depression: Uncertain Promise*. New Haven: Yale Univ., 1996.

"William Mitchell Journal." YMHA, 92nd Street Y Archives.

———. 3 Sept. 1898. YMHA, 92nd Street Y Archives.

———. 21 Sept. 1898. YMHA, 92nd Street Y Archives.

———. 21 Oct. 1900. YMHA, 92nd Street Y Archives.

"YMHA Athletics." *Y Bulletin* March 1913.

Young Men's Hebrew Association. *Twenty-Eighth Annual Report, 1902*. YMHA, 92nd Street Y Archives.

———. *Thirty-First Annual Report, 1905*. YMHA, 92nd Street Y Archives.

———. *Thirty-Fourth Annual Report, 1908*. YMHA, 92nd Street Y Archives.

———. *Forty-Third Annual Report, 1917*. YMHA, 92nd Street Y Archives.

YMHA Bulletin Nov. 1900.

———. Dec. 1900.

———. Jan. 1901.

———. Jan. 1902.

———. May 1907.

From Suburbanites to Sabras and Back: How Jewish Americans Established Lacrosse in Israel

by Neil Kramer

Israel made a smashing debut at the 2014 World Lacrosse Championship in Denver, finishing seventh overall out of thirty-eight teams, with a 6–2 record. The team's two losses were each by a single goal to Australia and England, both of which have been playing the sport for a century and have competed in every World Games since 1967 ("Israel Rallies past Japan"). According to the "lacrosse news website laxpower.com," which publishes exacting quantitative analyses of lacrosse results, Israel's performance ranked fifth in the field, based on comparative scores and strength of schedule ("Computer Ratings for Teams in the FIL World Championships").

Whether fifth or seventh, the 2014 results of Israel's team, composed of men, who learned lacrosse in the United States, raises the question of how Jews came to be so proficient in this sport? While the story of Israel's lacrosse team is recent, its players would not have been so successful at the World Lacrosse Championship had there not been a cadre of excellent American Jewish lacrosse players and coaches. Thus, the story of Israel Lacrosse in 2014 has two major components: the story of the Israeli team, itself, and its origins in decades of Jews having lacrosse success in America.[1]

Lacrosse originated with the native peoples of North America. Europeans first encountered it during colonial times and adopted the sport in the mid-nineteenth century, after which it continued to have a limited following in the US, Canada, Australia, and the British Isles. Until the mid-twentieth century, lacrosse was overwhelmingly limited to elite prep schools, the nation's military academies, and some of the more selective colleges and universities in the northeast.[2] Because lacrosse requires a large playing field for practices and games (current dimensions are 110 yards by 60 yards) with enough surrounding buffer space so that errant shots and passes do not damage structures, windows, or passersby, it has been a sport played in suburban locations much more so than in cities with little open space such as New York or Philadelphia.

Israeli Lacrosse got started due to the efforts of a young New Yorker, Scott Neiss ("Scott Neiss"), as a product of his 2010 Birthright experience—through which he along with thousands of other Jewish young people from all over the world have received a free trip to Israel so they can learn more about the country and its relationship to their Jewish heritage ("About Taglit-Birthright Israel"). At the pivotal moment of reflection to those young Jewish men and women who have come to visit Israel, often for the first time, the Birthright trip leaders pose a fundamental question, "What are you going to do for the Israel you have just encountered?" Scott Neiss answered, "I'll bring lacrosse to Israel." Then a young executive, who had worked for several American professional lacrosse leagues, now a Tel Aviv resident and Israeli citizen, Neiss recruited coaches and players with World Championship experience and established lacrosse training centers in Israel. He also combed the country for *Aliyah*-niks (that is, recent immigrants to Israel) who had played the sport in North America, established Israel Lacrosse as the national governing body for the sport, and raised the financial resources (more than $700,000) to enable Israelis to compete at the highest levels of the sport. Unlike Tal Brody, the American basketball All-American who led Israel to the European Cup Championship in 1977 ("Tal Brody"), Neiss is not a very proficient lacrosse player; instead, he led from the sidelines rather than the playing field.

A year after Neiss's initial Birthright experience, I went to Jerusalem to referee "the first ever lacrosse match on Israeli soil," as the advertising poster for the game declared. In July of 2011, Larry Turkheimer, a Los Angeles businessman (and one-time lacrosse All-American at the University of North Carolina), enlisted me and Jeff Alpert, then a UCLA student, as a *l'dor v'dor* (that is, "generation to generation") refereeing duo (I was sixty-three then, Jeff was twenty-one). Maybe "draft" is closer to Larry's approach than "enlist." "Israel has just been admitted to the Federation of International Lacrosse (FIL), even though there's never been a game played there. The first game is next month and they need a ref. You're a teacher. You've got the summer off. Use some frequent flier miles and do the game." So I figured that if an international sports governing body had admitted Israel without bureaucratic fuss or any global political nonsense, and it was the governing body of the sport in which I had more than four decades of experience, then I'd better go and do the game.

Why was Israel admitted to the FIL in the first place with so little experience or infrastructure in lacrosse? This wasn't a gesture of philo-Semitism; rather, it happened because of the FIL's pragmatic desire for international expansion. Indeed, Israel was not the only country with an infant lacrosse program that was embraced by the FIL. It also reached out to similar fledgling programs in Hong Kong, Bermuda, and Thailand. Estonia, Russia, and Uganda are examples of the FIL's associate members ("Members by Member Type").[3]

Fast forward to July 2014. Jeff and I received a similar offer to serve as referees, but this time to officiate Israel's pre-tournament games immediately before the World Championships in Denver, Colorado. The Israeli team, like all national teams, was assembled specifically for this quadrennial event. The pre-tournament games, as well as games at the Vail Invitational over the July 4th holiday and during a preceding Birthright Lacrosse pilgrimage in June, provided the setting for player selection and also served to facilitate the building of team cohesion ("Israel Shocks No. 10 Sweden"). Whereas the 2011 game in Jerusalem had been ragged at its best moments, the 2014 Israel contingent in Denver, comprising two teams—designated "championship" and "development"—along with coaches, managers, trainers, photographers, and an entourage of parents, siblings, and other supporters, showed how far Israel lacrosse had come in less than three years.[4]

The rules for international lacrosse differ enough from those of the American collegiate game, with which the Israel team members (including coaches) were most familiar, that Neiss tasked Jeff and me with helping the players learn the international rules ("A Table of Differences").[5]

Israel's first pre-tournament game in Denver pitted the team against the Iroquois Nationals, whose Native American ancestors, as noted above, created the sport millennia ago. Although the two teams did not meet in the tournament—the Iroquois finished third and Israel was seventh—their first scrimmage demonstrated convincingly that Israel could compete against the teams in the tournament's power pool.

That first scrimmage was our introduction to the 2014 Israel team. After the scrimmage with the Iroquois, Jeff and I remained on the playing field and answered the Israeli players' questions about the rule differences. We expected them to view us as partners in preparation for the tournament, in part because we wore referee striped shirts with an Israeli flag patch above the left pocket, instead of the Stars-and-Stripes patches we wear when working games in the

US. Those Star of David flag patches did not inhibit the Iroquois players from joining our informal post-game rules seminar. What mattered most was the competence Jeff and I had shown on the field in administering the international rules, not the symbols on our shirts. This was all the more remarkable since many of the Iroquois players had extensive experience with the international rules, having played in under [the age of]-nineteen competitions; and some of them were coming off fabulously successful seasons in American college lacrosse. Two of the Iroquois players, brothers Lyle and Miles Thompson, had shared the 2014 Tewaaraton Trophy as the best college players in the land (*The Tewaaraton Award*).

The Israeli players, more than half of whom are now full-time residents of Israel, concentrated on their competitive responsibilities during the games, but the tumult arising from the most recent Gaza conflict was never far from their thoughts. Neiss set the tone with a message to the team and its supporters on the eve of the international competition:

> ... we press forward, and continue onward with our mission to bring joy to the communities of Israel through sport during this difficult time. Our youth camp has continued this week despite threats in Tel Aviv. We've scholarshipped children from the South of Israel who have been relocated to the center, away from the border with Gaza. We will continue with our lacrosse camp in Ramla next week unless the IDF's [Israel Defense Force's] Home Front Command Unit instructs otherwise. It's with this attitude that we press forward, and make our debut in the World Games.... We will not be deterred.

Since the Israel players have roots in the United States, their connections to the site of the World Games may explain some of Israel team's success. But no level of emotional attachment or organizational competence will prevail in the absence of talented and experienced players who are well coached and well led.

As previously noted, many Americans tend to view lacrosse as a niche sport. The word "lacrosse" may be associated by most Americans (even those who are sports fans) with a line of Buick sedans, rather than a ball-and-stick field sport. Those slightly better acquainted with the sport may know that football great Jim Brown was a lacrosse star at Syracuse University in the 1950s. Nonetheless, in the twenty-first century, lacrosse has spread rapidly. In fact, lacrosse has become the fastest growing team sport in America since 2001, with a seventy-percent increase in the number of high schools offering boys' lacrosse. Lacrosse now rates fifth among team sports (after football, basketball, baseball, and soccer) in high school student participation, with a 155 percent increase in participation from 2001 to 2014, that statistically overshadows the participation growth in basketball (0.2 percent), baseball (7.1 percent), football (8 percent) and soccer (25.4 percent) ("2014 High School Lacrosse Sponsorship").[6]

While there are no official statistics that track religious identity against participation in particular sports in the United States, Jews appear to be disproportionately numerous among the most accomplished lacrosse players. Notably, two members of the US national team, Jesse Schwartzman and Max Seibald, are Jewish. Schwartzman has been recognized twice as the most valuable player in the NCAA championships and has the most wins of any goalie in Major League Lacrosse. Seibald was the 2009 winner of the Tewaaraton Trophy.

A number of successful Jewish lacrosse veterans rallied to the Israel team. Head coach Bill Beroza was captain of the winning US team in the 1982 World Championships ("William S. Beroza"). Defensive coach Mark Greenberg was his teammate in 1982, when he was recognized with a spot on the tournament's "all-world" team ("Mark J. Greenberg"). The team's development director, Larry Turkheimer, was an All-American at North Carolina ("Larry Turkheimer"). Howard Borkan, the team's general manager, played at Cornell and is a multiple honoree of the Long Island Metropolitan Chapter of US Lacrosse, the sport's national governing body ("Howard Borkan").

Besides these leaders, there are veteran players on the Israeli National Team, who originally played on American college and in some instances professional teams. Midfielder Ben Smith is assistant coach at Harvard, where he also played as an undergraduate. Back-up goalie Reuven Dressler is a forty-one-year-old Tel Aviv physician who starred in the NCAA tournament while at Yale. Attackman Ari Sussman, who played collegiately at Dartmouth, and midfielder Casey Cittadino from Towson State University in Baltimore, are veterans of Major League Lacrosse, the fourteen-year-old professional league started by Jake Steinfeld, a Jew from Long Island, NY, whose brief collegiate lacrosse career at Cortland State in New York preceded a successful Hollywood career, first as an actor and personal trainer, later as an entrepreneur and philanthropist (Rosenfeld).

Still, we may well wonder how lacrosse became such an attractive sport-of-choice for Jews, first in America and more recently in Israel? Why have Jews had success in a sport normally associated with Native Americans, prep schools, Ivy League universities, and the service academies? When, why, and how did lacrosse become, if not *the* new Jewish game, certainly a game in which Jews are notably successful?

As noted above, lacrosse has experienced explosive growth in the twenty-first century. When it comes to Jewish interest in this sport, among the several factors to be considered is geography. For example, on Long Island, NY, which has a disproportionately large Jewish population compared to the rest of the country, lacrosse had already started on its growth spurt in the mid-to-late twentieth century. For this reason, the number of boys' high school teams on Long Island increased only from ninety-three to ninety-seven between 2005 and 2014. By comparison, in the rest of New York State over the same decade boys' high school lacrosse grew by 32.9 percent. In the seven states (and also including the District of Columbia) with the greatest Jewish population in 2010, (California, Florida, Illinois, Maryland and DC, Massachusetts, New Jersey, New York, Pennsylvania), high school lacrosse grew by 46.3 percent (49.9 percent if Long Island is excluded). These eight states accounted for seventy-two percent of the US Jewish population in 2010. In the other forty-two states, comprising twenty-eight percent of Jewish population but 60.5 percent of total population, lacrosse in high schools grew by 64.2 percent from 2005 to 2014. These data support the conclusion that lacrosse had its deepest penetration into American sports, at least as measured by the number of high schools offering the sport, in those parts of the country with the greatest proportionate number of Jews.[7]

As noted, this has been particularly so on Long Island. For many Jewish families, Long Island was the suburban escape path from New York City during the post-World War II period; so baby boomers and their children grew up in a locale where lacrosse had begun to take root. Other regions of concentrated lacrosse development in the mid-to-late twentieth century, such as the Boston and Baltimore-Washington suburbs, also had significant Jewish populations. At the World Lacrosse Championship in Denver, there were several instances in which the players' fathers would introduce themselves to me and recount the stories of their lacrosse careers. Overwhelmingly, these stories were told in the distinctive regional speech of Long Island's Nassau and Suffolk Counties, with an occasional voice having a Baltimore accent.

Hence, despite being thought of as a sport with Native American origins, a favorite of tony prep schools, an Ivy League college specialty, or a sport with deep roots at the nation's military service academies, lacrosse has also turned out to be attractive as a path to assimilation for the children and grandchildren of Jewish immigrants. The settlement houses and YMHAs of the Lower East Side did not sponsor lacrosse (though some of their latter day successors do in this decade). As Ari Sclar has shown elsewhere in this volume, those institutions sponsored basketball (also boxing) as an activity to promote American values of fitness and manliness. But for the next generation of American Jews, and specifically those who moved from city to suburb, and who might wish to immerse themselves in an identifiably American activity through which their immigrant legacy might be shed, or at least de-emphasized, lacrosse provided a superb vehicle for assimilation. Like any process involving people with dissimilar backgrounds and traditions, American Jews who took up lacrosse encountered all sorts of reactions from their teammates and competitors: embrace, anti-Jewish remarks, prejudice affecting game participation, or simply being treated as just another player on the team. For those who could not safely or confidently proclaim their Jewish identity, the success of Israeli lacrosse, though a generation removed from their own experiences, led some of the parents and other supporters of the team to see it as a reversal of the hard memories they had from unpleasant moments in their athletic careers.

The athletic requirements of lacrosse may also have contributed to the engagement of American Jews with the sport. Speed, skill, and power are essential attributes in virtually every athletic endeavor, though not in similar proportions. Lacrosse players tend to be significantly lighter and shorter than their counterparts in football and basketball, for example. Note, in this respect, a comparison of the 2014 rosters for the three sports at Duke University—the 2014 NCAA Division I lacrosse champion, but also an institution with successful teams in the other sports: Lacrosse participants, on average were 4.8 inches shorter than their basketball counterparts and forty-one pounds lighter than their football brethren. Since the lacrosse team averaged six foot, one-half inches in height and 188.8 pounds in weight, these were not small or slight men (though thirteen out of forty-five players on the roster were under six feet tall and fourteen weighed less than 180 pounds). In comparison to football and basketball, however, lacrosse would appear to be more egalitarian in terms of size and mass.[8]

The absence of a professional field lacrosse league for most of the twentieth century and its paltry salary level when once established (less than $20,000 per season for most players in 2014) tended to support the participation of Jews in lacrosse in two ways. Those athletes who sought a substantially more remunerative career in sports tended to try other activities—baseball, football, tennis, golf, basketball—limiting to a considerable extent the number of transcendently gifted athletes playing lacrosse and thus enabling Jews to have an increased potential for success.

In this respect, the experience of Jim Brown, the famous football Hall of Famer mentioned in passing above, is illuminating. Not only was Brown a virtually unstoppable force in college football before turning professional, he was likewise impossible to overcome in lacrosse. Predictably, after college he chose to play football due to its earning potential. Still, more than once he remarked that he played football for money, but preferred lacrosse as a sport. Brown's after-sports career may more subtly illuminate another aspect of why lacrosse may appeal to Jews. After he left football for work in film, Brown also engaged himself for long years in social justice campaigns. Thus, both professionally and personally, he sought a life that had a greater meaning beyond the narrow confines of the playing field. Jews in a similar fashion have never tended to look at the pursuit of sports and the fame and money it might earn them as their ultimate goal. Other values have always been deemed to have greater significance—especially the well-known emphasis on higher education in Jewish families. Hence, the absence of a professional life in lacrosse was not a disincentive for young Jews who wished to make it their sport of choice (McLaughlin).

The prevalence and popularity of lacrosse at prestigious colleges and universities contributed to athletes' family support of lacrosse. Whether Ivy League or Little Three (Amherst, Wesleyan, Williams), lacrosse has had a home at the sort of colleges striving Jewish families hoped their children would attend. Even though lacrosse is as rugged as the other male sports (though not as physically dangerous as football, by any means), the likely options for continuing a high school lacrosse career into college were much more attractive to aspiring Jewish families in terms of higher education attainment and social value than many of the universities offering football, basketball, and baseball.

All of these factors contributed to American Jews' embrace of lacrosse and by extension contributed to Israel's success at the 2014 World Lacrosse Championships—thanks to Israeli players who learned the game in the United States. Those factors have operated for many years and have created a critical mass of Jewish athletes and coaches accomplished in lacrosse, upon which Israel will continue to be able to draw for the foreseeable future. There is no reason to expect that this circumstance is likely to change much in the years ahead, even though the future growth rate for lacrosse participation in the United States most likely will be in states with a relatively smaller proportion of Jews. This reflects the case noted above for Long Island in macrocosm. That is, since lacrosse has already deeply penetrated most of the areas where Jews live, the most likely areas for the sport's further growth are beyond those enclaves. One might idly speculate whether lacrosse could ever become a multi-billion-dollar sports cartel like the National Basketball Association or the National Football League with Scott Neiss (at least in Israel) becoming the next David Stern or Pete Roselle. Probably not. Far more likely, lacrosse will remain a niche sport for suburban and prep school athletes who are not aspiring to a multi-million-dollar professional sports career (however illusory those aspirations may be). It will continue to attract athletes of all sizes and shapes, creating a far more athletically egalitarian cohort of players. Highly accomplished players will find their collegiate athletic opportunities concentrated at institutions that genuinely expect athletes also to attend to their studies. In sum, Jews will continue to choose lacrosse and excel at it for the reasons that have prevailed for much of the late twentieth and now into the early twenty-first century.

Moreover, beyond the obvious benefits for Israeli lacrosse, there may be a benefit for American Jewish culture as well. In fact, the comprehensive growth of programs to support Israeli Lacrosse has the potential to work both ways—not only as a benefit for Jews in Israel but also as a benefit for Jews in America. It is important to note the establishment of lacrosse in Israel does not end with the national team. The same people who brought lacrosse competition at the highest level to Israel have also led the development of lacrosse programs for Israeli children (both Jewish and Arab). A program in Ashkelon, the centerpiece of Neiss's organizational efforts, has been on the leading edge of an effort that involved one thousand children in the summer of 2014 ("U.S. Volunteers Stick Out Conflict"). Part of the staffing for those lessons has come from forty participants in a lacrosse-themed Birthright trip that took place in June 2014. Equally divided between men and women, the "Lacrosse Birthright" participants were all active lacrosse players in college varsity programs. The trip sought to use lacrosse as a platform to educate, engage and energize various Israeli communities while gaining a better understanding of what Israel and the region have to offer in sports. As Neiss notes:

> We're big believers in using sport as a platform to help connect [American] Jews with Israel. Many players with aspirations to compete at the NCAA level are justifiably so focused on training and attending recruiting camps, so Israel takes a backseat. This is a great opportunity for Jewish athletes to take a free trip to Israel, while spreading their passion for the game internationally. ("Lacrosse Players to Tour, Teach and Train")

The upshot of this engagement of American Jews in a Birthright lacrosse program will undoubtedly have a rebound effect. Neiss and his fellow Jewish lacrosse enthusiasts and players desired to bring lacrosse to Israel as a direct response to the Birthright challenge: What can you do for Israel? But, in doing this, they have also brought a deeper connection with Israel back to a dedicated cadre of American Jewish athletes. In view of the origins of lacrosse with the Iroquois and other North American indigenous peoples, it may be fitting to speak of a transfer from America's equivalent of a deeply engrained culture to the native-born *sabras* of Israel that then bounces back to America's Jewish athletes with profoundly enriched understanding of and engagement with Israel.

Notes

1. This analysis does not address women's lacrosse. Women's and men's lacrosse are distinct sports that share a name and some of the same equipment.
2. On the Native American origins of lacrosse, see Conover. For a more detailed study, see Vennum. For more recent developments, see McPhee.
3. In a forum-post about adding lacrosse as an Olympic sport, Steve Stenersen (who has been the President and CEO of US Lacrosse since its founding in 1998 and was executive director of its predecessor since 1984) revealed the motive for international expansion: obtaining public funding for lacrosse in the rest of the world:

   > However, IOC [International Olympic Committee] recognition of lacrosse would be game-changing for the sport's international development. The ability to associate lacrosse with the five rings would bring instant credibility to the sport in developing lacrosse nations and likely qualify lacrosse governing bodies for public/governmental funding . . . in all nations except the US, of course, because the USOC [United States Olympic Committee] and its member NGBs [National Governing Bodies] receive no direct public support. The FIL has already been accepted as a member of SportAccord and the International World Games Association, which are closely allied with the IOC, and high ranking officials from both of those organizations, as well as the World Anti-Doping Association, attended the world championship in Denver.

4. According to Bill Beroza, head coach of the "championship" team, and Pete Ginnegar, head coach of the "development" team, the championship team comprised the top twenty-three players who were eligible according to FIL regulations. The development team comprised players who were younger, often still living in the USA without a fully developed commitment to living or working in Israel, or who were not as accomplished as the top twenty-three. Some of these younger players on the development team—young men still in high school or early into their college careers—might have made the championship team, but they or their families were not ready to make the kind of commitment to Israel (including possibly service in the Israeli Defense Forces) that might have arisen from meeting the FIL eligibility requirements.
5. The rules differences are overwhelmingly technical—timing factors (running time rather than the stop time system used in the US), penalty administration, penalty enforcement with regard to the sequence of penalties, size of teams (limit of twenty-three), stalling—but the devil is in all the details. While not part of our story, the outcome of the championship game between the US and Canada was determined in part by the failure of the US coaches to understand how the FIL timing factors and

stalling rules dictated a different tactical response than would have been successful in the US college game.
6. The source for these data are from the National Federation of State High School Associations, the range of whose membership is limited and does not include approximately 1250 boys lacrosse teams and 650 girls lacrosse teams. So, if anything, these data understate the growth of lacrosse.
7. Census data came from census.gov. High school lacrosse participation data came from "High School Participation Rates." Jewish population data came from Dashefsky and Sheskin.
8. Rosters were accessed from *GoDuke.com*. While it is often the case that height and weight information on athletic team rosters are notoriously unreliable, using data from a single institution allows for an analysis, in which we can hope that inaccuracies and exaggerations are consistent for all sports.

Works Cited

"2014 High School Lacrosse Sponsorship and Participation Rates." *Laxpower*, 8 Sept. 2014. 18 Sept. 2014 <http://www.laxpower.com/laxnews/news.php?story=40892>.

"About Taglit-Birthright Israel." *Taglit-Birthright Israel*. 18 Sept. 2014 <http://www.birthrightisrael.com/TaglitBirthrightIsraelStory/Pages/default.aspx>.

"Computer Ratings for Teams in the FIL World Championships." *Laxpower*, 27 July 2014. 18 Sept. 2014 <http://www.laxpower.com/laxnews/news.php?story=40749>.

Conover, Adele. "Little Brother of War." *Smithsonian.com*, 1 Dec. 1997. 17 Aug. 2014 <http://www.smithsonianmag.com/people-places/little-brother-of-war-147315888/?no-ist>.

Dashefsky, Arnold, and Ira Sheskin, eds. *American Jewish Year Book 2012*. Dordrecht: Springer, 2013.

GoDuke.com. 18 Sept. 2014 <http://www.goduke.com>.

"High School Participation Rates." *Laxpower*. 18 Sept. 2014 <http://www.laxpower.com/common/ParticipationRates2014.php>.

"Howard Borkan." *Israel Lacrosse*, 3 Jan. 2000. 18 Sept. 2014 <http://www.lacrosse.co.il/2000/01/howard-borkan/>.

"Israel Rallies past Japan to Secure No. 7 World Ranking." *Israel Lacrosse*, 19 July 2014. 17 Aug. 2014 <http://www.lacrosse.co.il/2014/07/israel-rallies-past-japan-to-secure-no-7-world-ranking/>.

"Israel Shocks No. 10 Sweden, 19–4, to Open 2014 World Championship." *Israel Lacrosse*, 11 July 2014. 18 Sept. 2014 <http://www.lacrosse.co.il/2014/07/israel-shocks-no-10-sweden-19-4-to-open-2014-world-championship/>.

"Lacrosse Players to Tour, Teach and Train with Birthright-Israel This Summer." *Philly Lacrosse.com*, 26 Jan. 2014. 18 Sept. 2014 <http://phillylacrosse.com/2014/01/26/lacrosse-players-tour-teach-train-birthright-israel-summer>.

"Larry Turkheimer." *Israel Lacrosse*, 3 Jan. 2000. 18 Sept. 2014 <http://www.lacrosse.co.il/2000/01/larry-turkheimer/>.

"Mark J. Greenberg." *USLacrosse*. 18 Sept. 2014 <http://apps.uslacrosse.org/museum/halloffame/view_profile.php?prof_id=286>.

McLaughlin, Corey. "An Interview with Jim Brown: Passion for the Game." *Lacrosse Magazine*, 31 May 2012. 17 Aug. 2014 <http://www.laxmagazine.com/mll/2011-12/news/053112_an_interview_with_jim_brown_passion_for_lacrosse>.

McPhee, John. "Spin Right and Shoot Left." *The New Yorker* 23 March 2009. 17 Aug. 2014 <http://www.newyorker.com/magazine/2009/03/23/spin-right-and-shoot-left>.

"Members by Member Type." *Federation of International Lacrosse*. 18 Sept. 2014 <http://filacrosse.com/members-by-type/>.

Neiss, Scott. "Safety and Security during Difficult Times." *Israel Lacrosse*, 10 July 2014. 17 Aug. 2014 <http://www.lacrosse.co.il/2014/07/safety-and-security-during-difficult-times/>.

Rosenfeld, David. "Jake Steinfeld: A Don't Quit! Story." *Westside People* March–April 2014. 17 Aug. 2014 <http://www.westsidepeoplemag.com/2014/03/jake-steinfeld-dont-quit-story/>.

"Scott Neiss." *Israel Lacrosse*, 3 Jan. 2000. 18 Sept. 2014 <http://www.lacrosse.co.il/2000/01/scott-neiss/>.

Stenersen, Steve. "Re: Lacrosse Should Be an Olympic Sport." *Laxpower*, 29 July 2014 <http://network.laxpower.com/laxforum/viewtopic.php?f=18&t=12259&st=0&sk=t&sd=a&start=20>.

"A Table of Differences between the Current NCAA and the Current FIL Rules." *Federation of International Lacrosse*, April 2014. 18 Sept. 2014 <http://filacrosse.com/wp-content/themes/sportedge/downloads/FIL_vs_NCAA_Rules_Matrix_April-2014.pdf>.

"Tal Brody." *International Jewish Sports Hall of Fame*. 18 Sept. 2014 <http://www.jewish-sports.net/BioPages/TalBrody.htm>.

The Tewaaraton Award. 18 Sept. 2014 <http://www.tewaaraton.com>.

United States Census Bureau. 18 Sept. 2014 <http://www.census.gov>.

"U.S. Volunteers Stick Out Conflict to Share Lacrosse Skills with Israeli Youth." *Haaretz* 15 Aug. 2014. 18 Sept. 2014 <http://www.haaretz.com/life/sports/.premium-1.610642>.

Vennum, Thomas. *American Indian Lacrosse: Little Brother of War*. Baltimore: Johns Hopkins Univ., 1994, repr. 2008.

"William S. Beroza." *USLacrosse*. 18 Sept. 2014 <http://apps.uslacrosse.org/museum/halloffame/view_profile.php?prof_id=23)>.

About the Contributors

REBECCA ALPERT is Professor of Religion at Temple University. Alpert was one of the first women to be ordained as a rabbi in the 1970s. She is author of several books on twentieth-century American Jewish history and culture, gender and sexuality, and Jewish ethics. As an extension of these interests, she has, over the past several years, developed an expertise on Jews and sport. She was the founding co-chair of the Religion and Sport Section of the American Academy of Religion. She created and taught a course on "Jews, America, and Sport" for undergraduates at Temple University. She has published several journal articles on Jews and baseball. Her major work in the field, *Out of Left Field: Jews and Black Baseball*, was published by Oxford University Press in June 2011. Her latest book, *Religion and Sports: A Case Study Book*, will be available from Columbia University Press in 2015.

LISA ANSELL is Associate Director of the Casden Institute for the Study of the Jewish Role in American Life at the University of Southern California. She received her BA in French and Near East Studies from UCLA and her MA in Middle East Studies from Harvard University. She was the Chair of the World Language Department of New Community Jewish High School for five years before coming to USC in August, 2007.

LINDA J. BORISH, Associate Professor in the History Department and Gender/Women's Studies Program at Western Michigan University, earned a Ph.D. in American Studies at The University of Maryland. Borish's publications in sport history, women's and gender history and American Jewish history include chapters in *Sports in Chicago*; *Jews and American Popular Culture*; *Sports and the American Jew*; *Jews in the Gym: Judaism, Sports, and Athletics*; and *A Companion to American Sports History* as well as numerous scholarly articles in the *Journal of Sport History*, *The International Journal of the History of Sport*, *American Jewish History*, and other entries. Borish co-authored *Sports in American History: From Colonization to Globalization* (Champaign, IL: Human Kinetics, 2008), with Gerald Gems and Gertrud Pfister. Borish was a Visiting Scholar at the Center for Jewish History (summer 2012) for research on her book project, *"Not Merely Confined to the Gymnasium": Jewish Women in Sport in American Culture, 1880–1940*. Borish is Executive Producer/Historian of *Jewish Women in American Sport: Settlement Houses to the Olympics*, a documentary Produced/Directed by Shuli Eshel (2007), in conjunction with Maccabi USA/Sports for Israel. She served previously as Co-Editor Book Reviews, *Journal of Sport History* and is a Research Associate for The Hadassah-Brandeis Institute.

JOSEPH DORINSON is a professor in the History Department at Long Island University, where he has taught since 1966. Dorinson has co-edited a book, Jackie Robinson: Race, Sports and the American Dream (Armonk, NY: Sharpe, 1999) with Joram Warmand, and has written numerous articles on a variety of subjects spanning his beloved borough of Brooklyn: Black heroes, sports, politics, humor, and ethnicity. He has organized conferences at LIU Brooklyn on Jackie Robinson (1997), Brooklyn (1998) and Paul Robeson (1998). During baseball's first "Subway Series" since 1956, Dorinson appeared on television (CNN, Fox News, New York One); was heard on the radio (NPR, WOR); and was profiled in the New York Times discoursing on blacks, "reds," baseball, and the American experience.

JEFFREY S. GUROCK is the Libby M. Klaperman Professor of Jewish history at Yeshiva University. He is author of *Judaism's Encounter with American Sports* (Bloomington: Indiana University Press, 2005).

NEIL KRAMER is dean of faculty emeritus at New Community Jewish High School in Los Angeles. He earned a PhD in History at Claremont Graduate School in 1978. A private secondary school educator for more than thirty years, he was on the professional staffs of the American Jewish Committee and the American Jewish Congress in the early 1980s, and has been an adjunct faculty member at the Ziegler School of Rabbinical Studies of the American Jewish University. Kramer has been a lacrosse player, coach, and official for more than forty years and was the head referee for the first lacrosse game played in Israel in 2011. He lives in Los Angeles with his wife Robin, who is the executive director of Reboot. They have three adult sons, all of whom played lacrosse.

ARI F. SCLAR teaches at the Ramaz Upper School in New York City and is an adjunct professor in the History Department at Hunter College. He has a doctoral degree in American History from Stony Brook University and his dissertation examined basketball's impact on American Jewish culture and identity in the first half of the twentieth century. He is on the Advisory Committee of the National Jewish Sports Hall of Fame in Commack, New York. Sclar previously was the Senior Research Consultant for the documentary film, *The First Basket* (produced and directed by David Vyorst; distributed by Laemmle/Zeller Films, 2008) and served as the Director of Content of the Jews in Sports Online web site, first at New York University and then at the American Jewish Historical Society.

BRUCE ZUCKERMAN is the Myron and Marian Casden Director of the Casden Institute and a Professor of Religion at USC, where he teaches courses in the Hebrew Bible, the Bible in western literature, the ancient Near East, and archaeology. A specialist in photographing and reconstructing ancient texts, he is involved in numerous projects related to the Dead Sea Scrolls. On ancient topics, his major publications are

Job the Silent: A Study in Biblical Counterpoint (New York: Oxford Univ., 1991) and *The Leningrad Codex: A Facsimile Edition* (Grand Rapids, MI: Eerdmans; Leiden: Brill, 1998), for which he and his brother Kenneth did the principal photography. Zuckerman also has a continuing interest in modern Jewish thought, often looking at modern issues from an ancient perspective. He most recently co-authored *Double Takes: Thinking and Rethinking Issues of Modern Judaism in Ancient Contexts* (Lanham: MD: Univ. Press of America) with Zev Garber and contributed a chapter to Garber's book, *Mel Gibson's Passion: The Film, the Controversy, and Its Implications* (West Lafayette, IN: Purdue Univ., 2006).

The USC Casden Institute for the Study of the Jewish Role in American Life

The American Jewish community has played a vital role in shaping the politics, culture, commerce and multiethnic character of Southern California and the American West. Beginning in the mid-nineteenth century, when entrepreneurs like Isaias Hellman, Levi Strauss and Adolph Sutro first ventured out West, American Jews became a major force in the establishment and development of the budding Western territories. Since 1970, the number of Jews in the West has more than tripled. This dramatic demographic shift has made California—specifically, Los Angeles—home to the second largest Jewish population in the United States. Paralleling this shifting pattern of migration, Jewish voices in the West are today among the most prominent anywhere in the United States. Largely migrating from Eastern Europe, the Middle East and the East Coast of the United States, Jews have invigorated the West, where they exert a considerable presence in every sector of the economy—most notably in the media and the arts. With the emergence of Los Angeles as a world capital in entertainment and communications, the Jewish perspective and experience in the region are being amplified further. From artists and activists to scholars and professionals, Jews are significantly influencing the shape of things to come in the West and across the United States. In recognition of these important demographic and societal changes, in 1998 the University of Southern California established a scholarly institute dedicated to studying contemporary Jewish life in America with special emphasis on the western United States. The Casden Institute explores issues related to the interface between the Jewish community and the broader, multifaceted cultures that form the nation—issues of relationship as much as of Jewishness itself. It is also enhancing the educational experience for students at USC and elsewhere by exposing them to the problems—and promise—of life in Los Angeles' ethnically, socially, culturally and economically diverse community. Scholars, students and community leaders examine the ongoing contributions of American Jews in the arts, business, media, literature, education, politics, law and social relations, as well as the relationships between Jewish Americans and other groups, including African Americans,

Latinos, Asian Americans and Arab Americans. The Casden Institute's scholarly orientation and contemporary focus, combined with its location on the West Coast, set it apart from—and makes it an important complement to—the many excellent Jewish Studies programs across the nation that center on Judaism from an historical or religious perspective.

For more information about the USC Casden Institute, visit www.usc.edu/casdeninstitute, e-mail casden@usc.edu, or call (213) 740-3405.

www.ingramcontent.com/pod-product-compliance
Lightning Source LLC
Chambersburg PA
CBHW060955230426
43665CB00015B/2216